The Guardsman

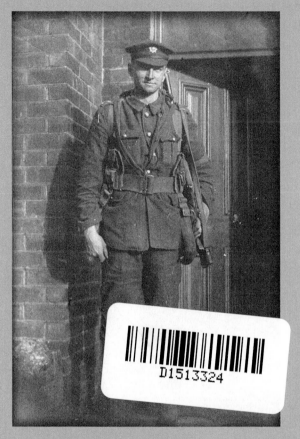

By Guardsman George Venables
Signaller in the 3rd Battalion Coldstream Guards
May 1915 – January 1919

Edited by Jamie Campbell

DayOne

Front cover image: Guardsman George Venables at the end of fourteen days' leave after the battles of the Somme and Passchendaele. Returning to the battle of Cambrai (Gouzeaucourt) December 1917. ©Venables Family.

The script for this book was originally collated and edited by Graham Hopkinson.

© Day One Publications 2019
ISBN 978-1-84625-650-9

British Library Cataloguing in Publication Data available

Joint publication with SASRA and Day One

Day One Publications
Ryelands Road, Leominster, HR6 8NZ, England
Tel 01568 613 740
North America Toll Free 888 329 6630
email sales@dayone.co.uk
web www.dayone.co.uk

SASRA
Havelock House, Barrack Road, Aldershot, Hants GU11 3NP
Tel 01252 310033   Fax 03000 302 303
Email admin@sasra.org.uk
web www.sasra.org.uk

Printed by T J International

Contents

Acknowledgements

SASRA is deeply grateful to Geoffrey Venables and to Graham and Margaret Hopkinson. Their vision and support in this project have been invaluable.

Endorsement

This is a gripping account of a young man caught up in the preparations for war and his subsequent experiences serving with a Guards Battalion on the Western Front of Europe in World War One. His story underlines the relentless and grinding nature of combat and the terrible toll it can take on those involved, both at the Front Line and at home.

Through the story we witness a man with a simple but strong faith. This faith gives him resilience and the strength to endure, despite personal grief and suffering. There are great acts of heroism and small acts of service recorded amongst the brotherhood of soldiers; but above everything, it's Venables' faith that helps him to be an encouragement to others in the midst of conflict.

Guardsman George Venables went on to influence the next generation of young people and never lost sight of the power of faith to give hope and strength. Over a hundred years on, the story of this soldier remains real and relevant to the challenges faced by the current generation of warriors and reminds us all that God answers those who call upon him.

Reverend Mark Grant-Jones
Senior Chaplain,
Royal Army Chaplains' Department

Foreword

Although Guardsman Venables was born in an era very different from our own, this book about his life and experience in war is both challenging and encouraging to us in our own time and I strongly recommend its reading.

Venables was brought up in a Christian home by parents whose godly life and influence rather than deterring him from following Jesus actually acted in a positive and decisive way. On leaving school he took up an apprenticeship in the building trade working eleven and a half hours a day for four shillings and sixpence a week. That must have taken a huge physical toll on him and yet he made time on Sundays to attend two services in church with Sunday School in between.

His solid Christian foundation proved its worth when Venables enlisted into the Coldstream Guards in 1915. The book paints a picture of the horrors of the First World War: the fragility of life at the front; the misery of the trenches; the joy of a few days' leave; the sorrow of losing dear friends. Indeed, Venables' own brother was killed in action. How easy it must have been to give up, to lose all hope and to fear for your own life and that of those around you.

The story of Venables' wartime service, however, is overarched and undergirded by his unshakable faith in the risen and ascended Lord Jesus Christ whose death and resurrection guaranteed his own resurrection and life eternal. Even in the midst of terrible carnage Venables found solace and comfort through the ministry of Miss Daniell's Soldiers' Home and the Soldiers' Christian

Association. His devotion to his Lord and Saviour was the lifelong priority of Guardsman Venables.

Colonel Edward Armitstead CBE,
late Coldstream Guards
Vice President SASRA

Sketch maps showing some of Guardsman Venables' locations between 1915 and 1919. © SASRA.

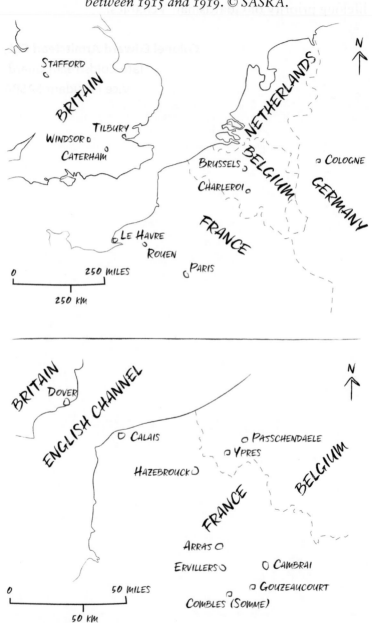

1. A Guardsman in the Making[1]

The childhood and boyhood of No. 16236 Guardsman George Venables passed quickly under the quiet influence of a deeply religious home life. Leaving Grammar School in his mid-teens, he commenced an apprenticeship to the building trade. He worked for eleven and a half hours a day. He earned four shillings and sixpence per week.

On Sundays he attended two services at the Plymouth Brethren's[2] meeting room and went to Sunday School in the

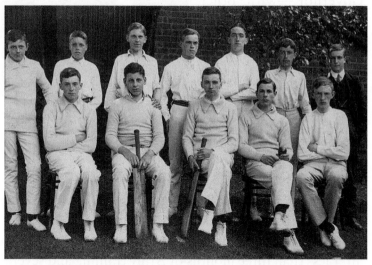

Schoolboy George Venables, front row, third in from the right. Captain of Stafford Grammar 1st XI.
©Source unknown—original with Venables Family.

---

1 The author writes about himself in the third person, in this book.
2 The origins of the non-conformist Plymouth Brethren date back to the early 19th Century. A number of its key speakers came from Plymouth in south west England.

afternoon. Under the gracious and prayerful guidance of wise and broad-minded parents he grew up to respect these influences which proved so irksome to many of his generation.

On his eighteenth birthday the ordinary routine of a busy and happy home life was suddenly broken by the outbreak of war. His elder brother—'the Governor'—with other schoolfellows joined the Coldstream Guards within a month. As the age limit for the Army was nineteen and most ordinary people expected the war to last no more than six to twelve months

Henry 'The Governor' Venables.
Older brother to George.
© Venables Family.

at most, Venables made up his mind that he would not be required for military service. But as time passed, the hope of an early peace receded.

The Governor and his companions were in action after less than three months of Army training and several were killed before Christmas. Venables began to realise he would have to decide about joining up. Like most Englishmen he had no desire to kill Germans and certainly no desire to be killed himself. War seemed to be utterly opposed to all his home training which was based on the teaching of the Lord Jesus and His Apostles. However, Venables was challenged. In Christ, he was ready for eternity; yet many combatants were not. In Venables' mind, failing to stand alongside these men in some way, was wrong.

Consequently, while his inclination was to join the Coldstream Guards, he felt the Royal Army Medical Corps would allow him to serve without taking life. Amidst his perplexity he quietly committed his way to God. God had never failed him at school. God must be trusted in the same way for the bigger things of life.

One Sunday morning in the middle of May 1915, a letter arrived from the Governor. It finished as follows: "I hear George is thinking of joining up. Tell him not to join the Guards—he couldn't stick it." The thought of his elder brother saying he could not stick it annoyed Venables, but the problem of a Christian taking life was still unsolved in his thinking.

The next morning, he went to the Recruiting Office, praying as he went.

"How old are you?" asked the Sergeant.

"Eighteen," he replied.

"Nineteen," shouted the Sergeant in a loud voice.

"Nineteen," said the Officer as he wrote.

"What do you want to join?" asked the Sergeant.

"Royal Army Medical Corps," Venables replied.

"Full up," said the Officer. "We do not want men for that Corps. "What's your next choice?"

"The Coldstream Guards" replied Venables.

"Is he tall enough?" said the Sergeant, not a little taken aback by such a complete change.

"Is he far enough round the chest you mean?" said the Officer, eyeing Venables' long lean figure. A tape measure was produced. Either the Sergeant's eyesight was dimmed by many campaigns or his fingers slipped as he pulled the tape, which read thirty inches.

"Thirty-three," he called out.

"He will do," said the Officer. "Report tomorrow for medical examination." The bigger things of life were becoming clearer!

Venables passed his medical examination. He took the customary oath and received the King's shilling. A week later, he was travelling to London on the afternoon express.

As he walked on to Charing Cross Station, he saw two tall fellows in khaki who evidently belonged to the Guards.

"Can you tell me if the train for Caterham goes from here?" he enquired politely.

"What! Another bloody young fool?" came the encouraging reply. "You might as well go to hell as go to Caterham. Anyway, we'll show you the way."

As the train journeyed south, they talked of the hardships and discipline of the Guards Depot. Venables learned the men had overstayed their leave and were a little sore at the prospect of the punishment to come.

The way to the Depot from Caterham Station was up a long steep hill. At the bottom of the hill Venables saw an encouraging signpost: it read, 'To Asylum and Barracks'.

After a few formalities in the Guardroom, an orderly took Venables through the Barracks and left him with the old soldier in charge of No.13 Hut in 'Tin Town'—a wartime extension of the Barracks.

As the old soldier instructed him how to make a bed of two trestles, three boards, three army blankets and a straw mattress, he said:

"You'll be all right if you do as you're told and behave yourself. If you don't forget the old soldier on pay day, he'll help you through."

A long row of similar beds stretched each side of the hut. The owners kept coming in, in twos and threes until the hut was full. They were a strange mixture of men who came from all parts of the country and from all walks of life. Suddenly the door at the end of the hut opened with a bang.

"Stand to your beds," yelled a voice of thunder. Every man jumped to attention and stood motionless at the foot of his bed. The Orderly Corporal and Barrack bully was about to call the roll. As he passed along the hut, he stuck his offensive face about two inches from one man, cursed the next and threatened another.

He came up to Venables, looked him up and down. The Corporal wondered what was coming to the Country to take such fellows into the Army and suggested Venables was more suitable for the Asylum next door. Peering into Venables' face with an oath, the Corporal said:

"We'll make a man of you. We'll lick you into shape. We tame lions here, remember."

Everyone remained silent, sullen and still, until he had gone. Then each pronounced his benediction on the Corporal in appropriate Army language. One after another they turned into bed. Venables could not face kneeling and praying before such a noisy company, so he slipped between the rough blankets in his shirt and pants.

"Put that light out," shouted the familiar voice of the Orderly Corporal as the bugle sounded the first note of lights out. "Stop talking will you." Darkness and silence reigned, broken only by sundry snores and groans from the thirty-five inhabitants of No. 13 Hut. At home, his father and mother were kneeling together, praying for their boys.

Venables had a 'letter of introduction' to a man called Mr Lance, who was the leading brother at the Brethren's meeting in Caterham. Venables' first day in Barracks led him to believe such a brother would prove useful, so at six o'clock in the evening he took his place at the end of a long queue of men waiting at the Barrack gate to go out.

Venables had been instructed in the ritual of getting out of Barracks by the old soldier in charge of his hut. Nevertheless, he felt considerably nervous as he stood clumsily to attention and repeated:

"No. 14 Company Coldstream Guards No. 16236 Private Venables."

The Sergeant eyed him up and down and looked at the long list of those confined to Barracks for various offences ranging from being untidy on parade to striking a Corporal. As Private Venables was not among them the Sergeant said, "Right."

Venables, a soldier with twenty-four hours' military experience, walked proudly out of Barracks to find Mr Lance, who was well known in the village and lived in a house called 'Barossa'. He approached the house through a beautiful garden in all the glory of the early June flowers. A girl with pigtails and pleasant smile opened the door in response to his ring.

"Does Mr. Lance live here?" he asked, "I have a letter of introduction to him."

"Come in," she replied, none too pleased at the prospect of feeding a hungry man on washing day when the ironing was still unfinished. However, the genial smile and hearty handshake of Mr Lance combined with the warm welcome of Mrs Lance put Venables at his ease.

Above left: Edward and Emily Lance. © Venables Family.
Above right: Ethel M Lance in 1915. She went on to marry George Venables on 3rd December 1927. © Venables Family.

The personnel who regularly visited the house were known as the 'Barossa Squad' and Venables was one of the first members. The squad grew as fresh recruits arrived and became a great influence for Christ in the Barracks.

By God's grace, this influence continued as they moved to further training at Windsor and then to battle.

The home of the 'Barossa Squad', Caterham.
Over 160 recruits from the Guards' Regiments signed the
visitor's book between 1915 and 1919. © Venables Family

King's Regulations stated that every man must wash and shave (except the upper lip) before breakfast. Shaving at any other time would not do. The order pertaining to the upper lip seemed likely to get Venables into trouble.

"You've shaved your top lip" said the Sergeant.

"I haven't, Sergeant."

"You've clipped it then," he yelled; his fiercely critical eye was about six inches from Venables' face.

"I haven't, I can't make it grow any quicker."

"Stop talking will you! My poor Regiment; what baby-faced kids they're sending us! Remember if you do shave your top lip, you'll stop in Barracks until it grows."

Breakfast was brought from the cookhouse by the swabs and served on a long table down the centre of the

*Guardsman
George Venables at
'Barossa', Caterham, 1915.
© Venables Family.*

hut. Each man had a thick rimmed pudding basin full of tea, a good big slice of bacon and bread divided out under the fatherly eye of the old soldier in charge. It was eaten in haste with constant urgings to, "Get a move on or the hut will never be ready for the Orderly Officer."

Then the swabbing began in real earnest. Table and benches were scrubbed, floors were dry-scrubbed with broken chalk and swept with soft brooms, basins and plates were washed and arrayed like soldiers. Tea buckets were polished to shine like a mirror. The stove, alas, was Venables' job. He thought the essence of 'black-leading' was to put plenty on, but to his dismay he found it had to be rubbed off before it would polish. There was black lead here, black lead there and black lead all over the hearthstone, which should have been white! It was all over Venables too.

"Put that bed straight! Who's on tea bucket? There's some chalk in the bottom of this one! Come on there, get a move on with the floor! The whole hut will be reported. What the bloody hell!"

The old soldier making his final urge to finish the swabbing stood opposite the stove, hearthstone, Venables and the black-leading. His astonishment turned to amusement.

"Here, get washed and straighten your bed and get on parade or you'll be in the clink. I'll finish it for you."

With this he got to work with the brush, muttering to himself. "Some blinkin' mother's darlin, or clerk, or summat I reckon."

When Venables returned from washing, all ready for parade, the stove shone with a perfectly black surface and reflected the spotless white of the hearthstone as though some miracle had happened.

Making ready for a kit inspection at the Caterham Depot.
© *Source unknown—original with Venables Family.*

He did not forget the old soldier on pay-day.

Under Sergeant M's training during the hot summer months Venables' muscles hardened, and his shoulders straightened. At this time, he learned the most important lesson of all for a soldier; to stand perfectly still, wait for the order and then obey smartly; or, as the Sergeant put it, "To stand still and wait for it and then move when you move." Venables also learned to look perfectly unconcerned and innocent as he was called all the foul names imaginable; it was an excellent discipline.

Shooting at the miniature rifle range was a pleasure; exercise in the gym was extra-strenuous; bayonet drill was revolting.

Sunday swabbing in the Guards' Depot at Caterham,
otherwise known as 'Tin Town'.
© *Source unknown—original with Venables Family.*

"In! Out! On guard," ordered the Sergeant, as they bayoneted bags of straw suspended from poles or prone on the ground.

"Come on there! Jerry will get you first if you don't move quicker—a saw tooth bayonet that pulls your guts out with it! Not very pleasant! When you've got your first man look out for the second. Remember it's harder to pull out than to push in."

"Charge!"

A row of sacks on a pole, representing men in a standing position were first attacked. "In! Out! On guard," ordered the Sergeant.

Then with clenched teeth they jumped into a trench to attack another row. "In! Out! On guard," they all shouted.

Next, a row on the ground representing men in the prone firing position. "In! Out! On guard!"

"Put your knee on his chest to get it out, it won't come out like that," yelled the Sergeant.

Later, Venables walked alone and prayed. "Lord may I never have to take life, but help me to do my duty." Sufficient for the day was the evil thereof in very truth;[3] yet, Venables believed that the Lord Jesus was sufficient too and could be trusted to help in the strange, mad, helpless world in which he found himself.

After dinner on Sunday the recruits were free to go out. Venables went to the Mission Hall where there was a Bible class for Guardsmen. Sometimes, he helped with the large Sunday School of over a hundred children. Afterwards, all the Guardsmen went to Barossa where they enjoyed a good tea followed by washing up and singing hymns. Later in the evening, they went to the 'Gospel Meeting' at the Mission Hall.

In the early days of the war very few men attended, but in the later years, when the Mission Hall was open every week night, the Gospel Meetings were often crowded with men.

One winter's evening the hall was full and hot and the men were physically tired after the week of parades in the frost. A very quiet speaker was saying that there were two companies present in the hall; the saved and the unsaved. Then he raised his voice with the challenge:

"To which company do you belong?" A big burly Scotsman woke from sleep and jumped to attention in the middle of the hall and called out in a loud voice:

"K Company, Scots Guards, Sir!"

---

3 Based on the Gospel of Matthew, Chapter 6 verse 34.

As Venables was getting into bed one Sunday evening the Corporal staggered in between two other NCOs (Non-Commissioned Officers). The Corporal was almost too drunk to speak. The NCOs undressed him and pushed him between the blankets on his bed. Venables fell asleep but soon after lights out sounded he woke with a start. There was a terrible uproar at the other end of the hut. Men were shouting and swearing, bed boards were banging and cracking in great pandemonium. He peered into the darkness as the confusion grew worse and wondered if they were murdering the Corporal.

Suddenly the door opened and the light flashed on as the half-dressed Orderly Sergeant entered the hut. The Corporal's supper of fish and chips had failed to settle on top of too much beer. Feeling sundry promptings of coming evil, the Corporal had risen and tried to make for the door by fumbling along the end of the hut. In the darkness and his half stupid state, he took the wrong direction, trod on the first man's chest, fell over the next two and deposited his fish, chips and beer on the next four.

The Sergeant first threatened to call the guard and put the whole hut under arrest. Then he hurried the much sobered and chastened Corporal into his own bunk, told the old soldier to clear up the mess quickly and put the light out before the Orderly Officer or the guard were alerted.

Next morning Hut No. 13 rose in a mutinous mood when Reveille sounded. They all smarted under a sense of injustice. The Corporal had escaped scot free, but if one of them had even dared to talk after lights out, he would have been reported. They resolved to report the Corporal and complain to the Captain. However, their intention did not receive approval from Sergeant M or other NCOs and, as Venables discovered, this stand-off was not quickly forgotten.

One morning after parade the old soldier said to Venables, "You're in the book for dirty boots."

When Venables arrived at the Company Office the Sergeant Major was arranging his prisoners, escorts, witnesses and men for leave. The air was electric. The Sergeant Major hustled the NCOs, the NCOs hustled the recruits.

"Tee Hun," yelled the Sergeant Major as the Captain, Orderly Officer and a young Subaltern came on the scene. The whole group sprang to attention. The Sergeant Major saluted. "Stand at ease! Stand easy," ordered the Corporal as all the men of importance disappeared into the Company office and banged the door.

In fact, the whole business went with a bang, illustrating the Army motto, "When you move, move. Or when you don't, stand still and don't blink an eyelid!" The proceedings appeared arranged to frighten the nervous to death, before they were condemned. There was a few minutes' tense silence and then the door opened.

"Private S," called the Orderly Sergeant.

"Escort and accused, tee hun! Quick march! Left right, left right, pick 'em up will you," ordered the Corporal in charge of the escort. They shot into the Orderly Room like a stone out of a catapult.

"Take his cap off," ordered the Sergeant Major.

Bang! The door was shut and silence reigned outside.

After a few minutes the door, the escort and the accused shot out as they had shot in and the prisoner's cap was jammed on his head as he passed the door.

"Privates S and Venables" called the Sergeant Major from inside. "Privates S and Venables! Tee hun! Quick march," re-echoed Sergeant M. "Left right, left right, left right!" Venables' eyes were fixed on the back of S's head as he banged his feet up and down in the approved style. The door banged and their feet were still going up and down like clockwork.

"Halt! Right turn!" ordered the Sergeant Major and they faced the Officers.

"Private S."

"Sir," said S as he took one pace forward.

"As you were," yelled the Sergeant Major as though he were drilling a Battalion. S took a pace back.

"When your name's called take a pace forward and *don't speak* until you're spoken to."

"S!" One-two went S's feet on the Orderly Room floor.

"Venables!" One-two re-echoed Venables' feet.

Venables gazed solidly at the window fastener opposite his nose. He could just take in with the corner of his eye the Captain, with the Orderly Officer on one side and the Subaltern on the other. The Sergeant Major was standing at the end of the table. There was a short and most impressive silence.

In a quiet, gentlemanly voice, the Captain read the charge and a dusty pair of boots became the issue at hand. This in turn revealed a dirty and untidy soldier—a terrible offence against Military Law.

Venables gazed at the window fastener as the Captain enquired into his past. Sergeant M said he was a well behaved and tidy soldier and the Sergeant Major said he was a good man on parade. The Captain turned to pass sentence. Venables' heart seemed to beat louder in the strained atmosphere. The Captain dwelt on the wickedness of dirty boots and expounded on the value of a clean sheet for a soldier and then added, "Admonished."

"Fall in! Right turn! Quick march!" Venables was again a free man with a light heart. As he walked to his hut, he hummed to himself. "What do you want with eggs and ham—when you get Tommy Tickler's jam. Form fours! Right turn—What do you do with the money you earn? Ho! Ho! Ho! What a lovely war." [4]

---

4 Based on part of the song called, 'Oh It's a Lovely War'.

2. A Guardsman in Training

In September 1915 Sergeant M's Squad passed out before the Adjutant and joined the other Squads necessary to make a complete Training Company. Venables said goodbye to his friends at Barossa and the Gospel Hall and left with a letter of introduction to Mr D, the leading brother at the Brethren's Meeting at Windsor.

Sergeant M's Squad, Coldstream Guards, August 1915.
Private Venables is standing in the back row, first on the right.
© Source unknown—original with Venables Family.

The Company proceeded to Windsor by train on a bright September afternoon and marched from the station to Victoria Barracks. The grey walls of the Castle towered above the road and the knowledge that before long he would be a sentry on its terraces gave fresh dignity to his calling.

The sleeping and living accommodation at Windsor consisted of long corridors divided into cubicles and

Venables shared his space with a Policeman from Shropshire. The Policeman, a family man well over thirty, persisted in smoking 'thick twist' in bed with the window shut. Venables was very thankful to share the privacy of a cubicle with a fellow who had so few objectionable habits.

The day's work usually commenced with a run before breakfast, in the Long Walk. Training consisted of Platoon and Company drill, night manoeuvres, route marches, field exercises in Windsor Park and rifle-shooting at Wraysbury. It was much more interesting than Caterham and all the men felt they were qualifying to be soldiers to help win the war, which was their sole purpose for their presence in the Army.

The first free evening, Venables made his way to France Road to present his letter of introduction. He was warmly welcomed by Mrs D who sent him to a Brethren Meeting in the Old National School. The Meeting had already started when he arrived. Between twelve and fifteen people sat round a table covered with a green baize cloth with their Bibles open. Just like the Prayer Meeting in Caterham, Venables knew he was amongst people who had a sincere reverence for Holy Scripture and a personal knowledge of God, as revealed in Jesus Christ. He returned to Barracks with a standing invitation to dinner on Sunday at Mr D's home, a request to take a Sunday School class and an invitation to tea every Sunday from Mr P. By these means, Venables formed the regular Sunday habit and a fresh connection with Christian homes and fellowship.

The first afternoon that was clear of duty Venables spent wandering round the Castle. He was charmed by the beauty and grandeur of all he saw. However, the view from the north terrace over Eton College and the Thames Valley, bathed in all the glory of Autumn colour and sunshine, was utterly at variance with the purpose that brought him there. Whenever he was confronted with the peaceful and beautiful, the problem of war and the questions relating to it continued to puzzle him.

He entered St George's Chapel in time for Evensong and, taking his place in the seats of the Knights of the Garter, with their banners overhead, he worshipped in the beauty of the Royal Sanctuary. The Bible reading, prayers and reverence stirred his soul. As prayers for the soldiers at The Front were said he thought of the Governor and wondered where he was and what he was doing.

Venables also visited the Soldiers' Home in Peascod Street, founded by Miss Daniell. The ladies who ran the home were very keen Christians and they were helped by Army Scripture Reader Ben Johnson[5] who visited the Barracks regularly and tried to bring the men to the home. He was an old, regular Coldstream Guardsman who had 'bad record' but was converted through the Christian witness of his Colonel some years before the war.

---

5 Benjamin Johnson joined the Army Scripture Reader and Soldiers' Friend Society in August 1903 and he left in January 1930. Born around 1869 in Liverpool, he died in January 1947. It was reported in The Flag in January 1915 that he and eleven other Readers had been sent to France in December 1914. Before becoming a Reader, Johnson served as a Guardsman in the 2nd Battalion Coldstream Guards (Dates unconfirmed). He married Clara Beams in 1892.

Army Scripture Reader Benjamin Johnson, centre row, first on the left. (Taken in May 1926 at HQ in London). © SASRA, Chapter Two of Sovereign Service *written by Brigadier Ian Dobbie OBE.*

On Christmas morning Reveille was sounded an hour later than usual and breakfast was followed by a voluntary Church Parade. The singing of carols and the message of peace and goodwill were strangely contradicted by the obvious war effort; but men believed it was a war to end war. While this was not an unreasonable hope, Venables was aware that many

Army Scripture Reader Ben Johnson, retired from his full time role with the Association on December 31st 1929. © SASRA.

men had no obvious concern about their eternal future. It saddened Venables to see the personal appeal of Jesus Christ was unheeded by the majority.

Later that day, Christmas dinner was served between half-past one and two. There was an ample supply of pork and beef, vegetables, Christmas pudding and beer. After dinner a collection was taken for the cooks, and the cookhouse closed. The only institution to remain open was the 'wet canteen'.

Venables retired to bed in the afternoon to sleep off the effects of his large meal. He felt very homesick as he thought of the family at home. He wondered what the Governor was doing in France and did not doubt his own lot was better than the Governor's.

His evening's peace was disturbed by the revellers returning from the 'wet canteen'. They were in various stages of intoxication according to the temperament of

Army Scripture Readers at the Front

OUR friends will rejoice to know that early in December, before going to press, we were able to announce that TWELVE Scripture Readers were out on service at the Front with the Expeditionary Force. These greatly-valued workers are appreciated by their former comrades more than any of us can imagine. The men love to have them in their midst, and invariably welcome them. The chaplains ask us for more than we can send out, and the cost of maintenance is very heavy. From our office in Paris we keep in touch with the military authorities, and though not able to publish the different stations or spheres of work of the Readers our friends will, we are sure, continuously remember them all at the throne of grace. Their names are:

J. R. Armstrong.
J. Billington.
Fredk. Burgess.
Chas. Coupland.
T. A. Evans.
G. J. G. Howard.
B. Johnson.
C. Lonney.
A. McEvitt.
Jas. Martin.
H. Morbey.
Robt. Oliver.
W. Ransley.
J. Walton.
B. Wood.

Extract from The Flag, January 1915. The report references the deployment of Readers to France at the beginning of December 1914. Army Scripture Reader Benjamin Johnson appears in the list of those deployed. © SASRA.

the individual and the quantity of beer consumed. Some were merry, some were cross and surly, some talkative and confidential; and some required assistance to bed. In this way, Christmas Day ended.

Having enjoyed a period of leave over New Year, Venables' training continued. As the months passed, warm sunshine began turning the Great Park from winter grey to the green velvet of spring and the daffodils were in full bloom in the Round Tower garden. Significantly, the Court was about to move to Windsor Castle for Easter and Venables' Company was selected to 'Find the King's Guard'.

Each day they practised changing guard and sentry on the Barrack square and twice they went through the whole ceremony in the Castle's quadrangle. It was an anxious time and three full evenings were spent preparing kit for the main event.

The best uniform was examined and all spots of grease and dirt removed. The best trousers were neatly folded with seams 'damped'. Knife edged creases came by using bed boards, a mattress and natural body weight.

Every piece of equipment was scrubbed; the brass tabs and fasteners were polished. Rifle and bayonet had special attention and boots and buttons were polished like mirrors. Topcoats were folded and carefully packed. Fingernails on the left hand were exemplary. The left hand held the rifle at the slope during inspection.

The morning the Guard was mounted the men made their final preparations. "Get dressed, the Guard," shouted the Orderly Sergeant at 9.30 am.

The men assisted one another to adjust packs and equipment; they pulled in their tunics and went to the parade ground. Here, everything moved with electrical precision and Venables' heart beat faster as the Officers' searching eyes examined him from top to toe but he breathed again as they passed. Then they came along the rear. It was a strange sensation to feel three men looking through him from the back but again they passed without comment.

"Close order march," commanded the Adjutant.

"Move to the right in fours! Form fours right! Quick march!"

The band struck up and they marched smartly out of the Barracks through the town and under the ancient archway to the Castle quadrangle, where the old Guard waited to be relieved. The green lawn, the grey walls of the Castle and the smartness of the Guard filled all ranks with Regimental pride.

By the end of April 1916 Venables' Company had completed its training and was expecting to be ordered to France. All hope the war would end before they went had gone and they were resigned to the inevitable.

One evening a notice appeared on Company Orders asking for volunteers to train as Signallers and Venables immediately sent in an application. The next day he was sent to the Signal Office for an examination in dictation and the following day he moved to the Signallers' Quarters. He said good-bye to the Shropshire Policeman and the remainder of his training companions. The following week they all left for France and he did not see them again.

Signalling work was far more interesting than anything Venables had done before and was accompanied by less red tape. He learned the alphabet in Morse Code by flag drill near Eton College and on the 'buzzer' in the Barrack room. After this, Venables and his companions were formed into a series of Signal Stations. They transmitted messages from one to the other by flag and heliograph during the day and electric lamp at night; speed and accuracy were essential. Additionally, they learned minor repairs to field telephones, various ways to repair cables damaged by shellfire and how to work small exchanges. The Spring and Summer days passed with variety and interest. (The following picture shows some of these skills being demonstrated by other Regiments in training.)

Troops of the 3/19th Battalion, London Regiment manning a Signal Station during training in the United Kingdom, September 1915. © IWM Q 053827.

At the Soldiers' Home Miss L left for a well-earned rest. She was replaced by Miss K. Miss K decided to invite to tea the men of the Coldstream Guards and the Horse Guards, who visited the recreation room. She thought it would be an added attraction if Venables spoke at the meeting following the tea. The tea was held, about half the men who had been invited turned up, half of those who turned up had urgent engagements after tea and left before the meeting. Only six of the men remained to hear Miss K's gospel talk.

Venables felt so sympathetic towards Miss K he promised to speak the following week. He took several walks in the Great Park with his pocket Bible, searched for a suitable text and planned to say quite a lot, but he felt sure that when the time came he would forget it all. He hadn't spoken at an event like this before.

When the evening arrived, he walked down Peascod Street and saw a large bill in the window of the Soldiers' Home. It read: **GOSPEL MEETING TONIGHT. Speaker PTE. VENABLES, Coldstream Guards**. Inside the bar there was another notice. Miss K had resolved to make the most of the occasion and for Venables there was no retreat!

He took his place behind a table in a state of nervous collapse and stared at twenty empty chairs. Miss K commenced to play and sing hymns but no congregation arrived. She went into the recreation room to invite the men, but they all had 'pressing engagements' and disappeared.

They sang another hymn and then Miss K broke her own rules and went downstairs into the coffee bar to try and persuade some to come to the meeting, but her efforts were unavailing. Venables was very relieved that there was no congregation and sat talking to Miss K.

"It is so very strange to get so few men in, Venables. You would think the men, knowing they so soon have to face death, would think of their souls." Venables agreed.

"If only we could get a number of keen men in the Barracks to bring others. There's Private J; he's saved but he won't kneel at night and pray in the Barrack Room. What do they say to you when you pray, Venables?"

"I don't kneel down. I wait till I'm in bed, pull the blanket over my head to shut out the noise and then I pray."

Miss K looked very grieved and a little shocked.

"Don't you think it would help others *and* show your colours if you did?"

"They know what I am all right," he replied.

"Yes, but Daniel prayed three times a day by the open window." [6]

"I could not pray with all the noise and swearing and everybody looking at me. In fact, I can pray best when I am walking alone in the Park."

Venables returned to Barracks, having promised to speak at the meeting the following evening on the understanding that the notices were removed. However, word had spread.

"I say Venables, I knew you were a Bible puncher, but I didn't know you were a Parson's son," said one of the men in his room.

"I should have come to hear what you had to say," said another; "only, I wanted my supper."

"He'll get it all knocked out of him in France," said a third.

"You stick to it, kid," said the Corporal. "It will stand you in good stead out there."

---

6 Miss K is referring to an incident in the Book of Daniel, Chapter 6 and verse 10.

The following morning as Venables walked onto the parade ground he saw a Squad of old soldiers being schooled by the Drill Sergeant and a youth fresh from Eton College with new uniform and one Officer's pip. His broken schoolboy voice contrasted remarkably with the Drill Sergeant's thunder.

"Now Sir," began the Drill Sergeant, "move the Squad to the other side of the square and leave them facing the Officers' Mess."

The youth thought for a moment then threw back his shoulders, lifted his head, took a deep breath and screeched, "Form fours!"

Not a man moved. The young Officer looked furious. His cheeks became crimson.

"No, not the men's fault Sir. They are all right. They will obey if you give the right command. Can't you see, they are standing at ease?"

"Platoon! Platoon! Tee hun! Form fours! Form two deep." Stand at ease!" he commanded and the men moved like clockwork.

"There you are Sir, they know what to do. Try again."

He tried again with more success and they marched smartly across the parade ground in fours. Then mistaking his right hand for his left, he wheeled them straight towards the Barrack wall.

"Look out Sir, they'll be over the wall and you'll lose the lot. Hurry up Sir, hurry up," said the Drill Sergeant. The Squad continued to mark time with the front rank right up to the wall.

"About turn! Right wheel!" yelled the young Officer.

"Now they're going into the canteen! Hurry Sir, hurry or you'll lose them! Quick, if they get inside, they won't come out," shouted the Drill Sergeant.

"Halt," bawled the youth as the front rank commenced to mount the canteen steps.

"Just in time Sir. Your right's your right and your left's your left in the Army Sir, whatever it may be in civil life. Now see how it's done."

With a few sharp words of command, he put the Squad exactly where he wanted it.

"Now Sir, move them back."

After dinner that day Venables hurried to the washing-up sink to clean his utensils before the water became cold and greasy. He succeeded in getting through the crowd that surrounded the sink without wiping his greasy plate on his tunic and without anyone else wiping theirs on his trousers. The water was hot and he was soon elbowing his way back with two clean plates, when a man who sometimes attended the Soldiers' Home tapped him on the shoulder and said:

"Come quickly to the other dining room. One of the new recruits from Caterham gave thanks before he ate his dinner."

They turned into the dining hall and Venables' friend led him to a middle-aged man who was just finishing his pudding. He turned out to be a member of the Salvation Army and promised to accompany them to the Soldiers' Home. They were very pleased to be able to take another man to the meetings to help restore Miss K's confidence in them.

3. The Battle of the Somme

During the first week of July 1916 the papers announced a great Allied Offensive on the Western Front designed to break through the German Armies and turn trench warfare into a war of movement. The civil population hoped it would be the beginning of the victorious end but the soldiers invalided from the Front were confirmed pessimists.

"Wait till the casualty lists are out. They won't think it's such a bloody fine offensive then," said the Corporal.

"A hundred yards of shell-blasted ground, no bloody use to anybody, a hundred good men blown to bloody hell and another hundred maimed and crippled, yet these armchair soldiers think the war's over, instead of just beginning," said another.

Battle of Albert. The ruins of Mametz, 4th July 1916.
It was captured by the British 7th Division on 1st July.
©IWM Q 000772.

A Chaplain writing a field post card for a wounded
British soldier near Carnoy. 30th July 1916.
© *IWM Q 004060.*

As Venables reflected on these conversations he had a persistent thought that his brother Henry had been killed. It was a feeling he could not shake off, so he determined to get a week-end leave and go home. The way from the station to his home was over a level crossing; his father usually met him there when he was expected on leave. Venables knew he would not be expected as he had been home the previous week-end, but as he approached the level crossing, he saw his father standing by the wicket gate; he was wearing a black tie. Venables knew at once that the Governor was dead.

"We've lost Henry. I'm glad you've come," said Venables' father. "Mother said you would come because she has been praying for you to come home."

"How is mother?"

"She's in bed; very brave but broken hearted."

"When did you hear?"

"There was a letter from the Front in a strange handwriting this morning. It was from one of Henry's comrades. They were fixing gas cylinders in the Front Line prior to an attack when a shell burst on the parapet of the trench and killed Henry instantly. We must be thankful he has gone to be with the Lord Jesus without suffering."

They were met at the door by his sister who hurried him to his mother's bedroom. He flung his arms round the broken-hearted woman and for some minutes neither spoke. Then she said, "Thank God he is with Christ, which is very far better, but it is hard to lose him. He was such a splendid son to me and big brother to you all."

Later, as Venables got into bed he thought of Henry's last words to him before he left for France: "Look after mother if I don't come back." The feelings Venables had controlled all day overcame him. Venables burst into tears and cried himself to sleep.

On Sunday morning he went with his father to the Breaking of Bread Meeting. On the way back, they met the Vicar of the Parish coming to express his sympathy with them before the morning service. There was one less to pray for by name and one more to add to the Roll of Honour.

Later, mother came down to dinner and in the afternoon busied herself completing the weekly parcel. Normally, this would be sent to Henry. Now Venables would receive it. As he left, she put her two hands on his shoulders, kissed him and said, "Good-bye. God bless you my boy," and disappeared quickly into the house.

Victoria Barracks was all astir for 800 men were to go to France to replace the 1,200 casualties the Regiment had suffered. Lists of men for France were published at the various Company Offices and Mr D and Scripture Reader Ben Johnson visited the Barracks; all 800 replacements received a 'Khaki Testament'.[7] Such was the size of the draft to be deployed, the full Regimental Band came down from London to play en-route to the station.

A few days later Venables returned to Barracks after a very happy evening and found his orders for France had been posted; he would leave in two days. He had been home the previous week-end. He was thankful he could not go again.

All surplus kit was handed in because from that moment his belongings had to be carried on his back. He said good-bye to the friends who had shown him so much kindness and on the last evening Miss L, who had returned to the Soldiers' Home, arranged a special tea and farewell Meeting. As the Meeting ended, there was a time of prayer followed by the singing of hymns; 'God holds the key of all unknown', 'I am glad' and 'God be with you till we meet again.'[8]

The upper deck of the troop ship was packed with other ranks of all Regiments. They had very little to say and seemed like men moving to some inevitable fate. When the boat was loaded, she put into the Solent and anchored off Netley Hospital until an hour or so after dark. It was a dark

---

7 Believed to be a reference to the Gospel of John, issued to all the troops.

8 References to well known hymns of the day.

night; not a light was to be seen on the fast receding shore and all the portholes of the ship were closed and darkened, to prevent the ship being seen by an enemy submarine.

The atmosphere below was unbearable, as it was the only place where smoking was allowed; the crowd, the smoke, the heat and the oily smell from the engines made Venables feel seasick. He selected a sheltered place on deck, wrapped himself in his greatcoat and with his pack for a pillow made himself as comfortable as his life-belt would permit.

In his tunic pocket he carried a pocket Bible, given to him by Miss K. His mother had written on the front page, "But without faith it is impossible to please Him, for he that cometh to God must believe that He is, and that He is a rewarder of them that diligently seek him." [9]

His father had written, "For ever O Lord Thy word is settled in heaven. Thy word is a lamp unto my feet and a light unto my path. The entrance of Thy words giveth light, it giveth understanding to the simple." [10] God and His Word were the two things to be trusted in the crazy chaos of the world.

Grey dawn was breaking across the sky and everybody on deck was beginning to move, when Venables stood up and stretched his limbs. The coastline of France was clearly visible and by the time the day had fully dawned they were entering the harbour at Le Havre. Beside the quay was the inevitable hospital ship. She was a thing of beauty with graceful lines, white paint and large red crosses. Beside her the little troop ship looked drab and dull.

---

9 The Letter to the Hebrews, Chapter 11 verse 6.

10 The Book of Psalms, Psalm 119 verse 105 and verse 130.

After a tiring uphill march from the docks, they arrived at Harfleur. It was a 'Caterham in France'; full of red-tape, hated by every self-respecting soldier but loved by a host of scroungers and staff, who made life unbearable for men passing through. When Venables' draft arrived, the Camp was empty except for the staff. All available men had been sent up to the Line to take part in the Somme Battle. Consequently, the newcomers were posted to their Battalions quickly, with Venables being allocated to the Third Battalion, Coldstream Guards.

Despite the fast posting, it was a hard slog to reach the Third Battalion. During these times Venables found himself inexorably drawn into an ominous, violent world. Travelling east, Venables saw the few remaining walls of Maricourt and Carnoy. Surrounding these sites were single shell-shattered trees, standing like skeletons. Further on,

A shattered tree in old trenches at the entrance to Maricourt, 24th September 1916. © IWM Q 078283.

Venables saw whole woods of broken tree trunks interspersed with mounds of bricks. The bricks had been villages. Trenches and wire entanglements stretched like scars in all directions; shell holes pitted the ground. Gloomily, the horizon offered no relief, either. Shells burst in clouds of black smoke and the whole landscape seemed to rock with the thunder of the guns as barrages were ordered and prosecuted. Large incongruous Balloons on both sides indicated key lines of engagement, as the combatants fought to gain the upper hand.

During his time in the ruins at Carnoy, Venables remembered Henry was buried nearby. When the soldiers' shelters had been finished, Venables walked out to Carnoy

Part of Carnoy Military Cemetery (Left) and the permanent headstone for Serjeant Henry Venables of the Royal Engineers, killed in action on 30th June 1916, aged 28.
© Venables Family.

Cemetery and commenced his search among the long rows of wooden crosses. He came to the grave of the Adjutant of the 3rd Battalion Coldstream Guards killed September 15th and in the next row he found a simple wooden cross which read: **Sergt. H. Venables RE. Killed in Action. 30th June 1916**.

A lump rose in his throat. Memories chased around his mind in quick succession. Venables remembered how the Governor had fathered them all; there was the last holiday in the Welsh mountains. Their plans to visit Scotland disrupted when war broke out: and now … pop, pop, pop, pop! A machine gun rattled out overhead! As Venables looked up, a German plane swooped down from behind a bank of white cloud onto a Balloon. The two observers jumped from the Balloon and their parachutes opened. At first it seemed as if the burning Balloon would catch them but it blew away. However, the aeroplane circled round and fired on the helpless men slowly descending to earth. With a heavy heart, Venables went back to the ruins of Carnoy.

The time of rest and re-equipping was over and in November, the Guards Division was to move back to the Forward Area. They proceeded by bus and a four-hour march to Citadel Camp near Meault.

The Camp was on a hillside well above the road and consisted of camouflaged bell tents surrounded by thick, slimy, chalky mud that stuck to everything. The tents were lit by candles on brackets on the tent poles and the only light available was the dim flicker that came from the tent doors. The weary men stumbled up the slippery slope to the tents and threw off their packs to rest.

The next day, the Battalion marched to A Camp which was situated amongst the shattered stumps of Trones Wood. This area was under shellfire so the billets consisted of holes in the ground about ten feet long by seven feet wide and eighteen inches deep, covered by bivouac sheets. Old trenches, barbed wire, redundant ammunition boxes, temporary graves, thick mud and shell holes full of water were obvious in all directions. They spent the day preparing to go into the Line.

General view of Trones Wood after a snow storm, November 1916. © IWM Q 001622.

When all was ready the following night, they sat round the bivouac drinking tea, or tea with rum, according to taste, and eating biscuits, margarine and jam. They laughed and joked but the flickering candlelight revealed anxious faces. Venables shared the general nervousness and prayed that he might come through and do his duty.

The moment had arrived. "Get dressed," came the sharp command from outside and they stumbled out into the darkness and formed up in Sections. When each Corporal had checked his Section and reported in, they were loaded with petrol tins of drinking water, bombs, flares and extra ammunition.

They moved off in single file through Trones Wood and up the hill in the darkness. The only guide was the dark form of the man in front and his repeated warnings of, "Mind the hole." "Mind the wire."

The flares from the line silhouetted the men in front as they crossed a ridge. They struggled on, slipping and stumbling through the mud until Venables heard voices in the darkness and saw the flicker of a lamp. He was wondering what it was when suddenly there was a vivid flash, a loud report and the scream of departing shells, as a battery of field guns fired.

"Fritz's supper," said the Corporal.

A few minutes later they arrived at the Support Line, which was an old German trench, containing a partially completed German dugout facing the wrong way. The entrance to the dugout was down ten steps and the roof was supported by wooden frames.

"No. 1 Section Headquarters," remarked the Corporal having posted his sentries. "Now a brew of tea Venables." Venables filled a mess tin with water from the petrol tin and the Corporal took out precious sticks from under his shirt and made a little fire which he kept feeding carefully to avoid smoke. When the tea was made Venables took a good drink, heaved, then rushed up the steps into the trench and was violently sick. Petrol was the most pronounced flavour, chloride of lime next; the taste of tea was absent.

The mail had arrived. When Venables opened his weekly parcel, he found a roast chicken, a piece of ham, a brown loaf, some home-made butter and a large slab of chocolate. He shared these provisions with his Section, giving the Corporal an extra large allowance.

After several days, Evening Orders announced that the Battalion was to bathe! The second hot bath in three months! Each Platoon paraded at intervals of a quarter of an hour with towel and soap, then marched to the Corps' baths beyond Meault.

The baths consisted of two well ventilated dressing rooms and a shower room. While one Platoon washed in the showers, the other Platoon undressed while the third changed its dirty underclothing for clean.

The concrete floor of the dressing room was wet, muddy and cold, so Venables stood on his dirty shirt while drying himself. When they were dry each man took his underclothes under his arm, put on his boots, trousers and tunic, then lined up in the biting east wind to hand in his dirty underclothes for new.

New socks, new pants, new vest. Splendid, thought the shivering Venables; but when he handed in his shirt the voice from inside the office labelled 'Shirts', said "Sorry chum, all the shirts are gone," and pushed back the wet and muddy shirt that Venables had offered in exchange for a new one.

"What's the use of clean pants and vest if I've got to put this lousy thing on again?" said Venables, much hurt.

"It's no use chum. There ain't any."

As Venables put on his wet, muddy, lousy shirt, he resolved not to stand on it the next time he bathed.

Venables was now employed as a Company Runner attached to the Company Sergeant Major, so while the Battalion spent the day preparing for the Line, he was running the Sergeant Major's errands. His boots were rather large and walking in the thick sticky chalk mud had rubbed his heel sore. He wondered whether to report sick but did not think his foot bad enough. He was afraid that everybody would think he was trying to avoid going into the Line, so he resolved to stick it out.

At 3.30pm on the 3rd December they commenced to march to the Line, with about a hundred yards between each Platoon. The ruins of Guillemont and Combles made for a bleak backdrop. During the march, the pain in Venables' foot became unbearable and in desperation he asked permission to fall out. This was at first refused. But the pain grew worse and he appealed again for permission, which was granted on condition that he followed on and reported to the Medical Officer at Battalion Headquarters. He was warned in no uncertain terms what would happen if the Medical Officer found nothing wrong.

Eventually, Venables arrived at Battalion Headquarters. He found the Officers' Mess and told the Orderly to report his arrival to the Adjutant who sent him to the Aid Post. When the Medical Officer came into the Aid Post he said in his sternest voice:

"What did you fall out for?"

"Sore foot Sir!" said Venables.

"Take your boot off."

Venables undid his boot hoping there was something to show, for only he could feel the pain. He pulled it off with difficulty and when he removed his sock it revealed a red, inflamed and very much swollen foot.

"Why did you not report sick before?" the Doctor asked. His look and tone of voice had changed and Venables' fears vanished.

"I haven't been in the Front Line before Sir and I did not like to dodge it. I thought I could manage."

"You ought to have reported sick before. Put a dressing on it Corporal. Give me a label. Send him back in the first ambulance. There's one outside now isn't there?"

"Yes Sir," said the Corporal as he tied the label the Doctor had written on Venables' buttonhole.

Without headlamps, the ambulance moved slowly to Combles. They drew up opposite some caves to collect any wounded from the Aid Post but finding none, proceeded up the hill and over the ridge to Guillemont. Here the driver stopped and with the aid of many matches and much swearing managed to light his lamps. In their dim flickering light and with the improvement of the road he quickened his pace and after much bumping, they arrived at the Corps Rest Camp, in Dives Copse. Venables thought of the others; wet, muddy and cold in the Front Line. Venables thanked God for the mercies of the day and was soon asleep.

The Medical Officer made his rounds early in the morning. On examining Venables' foot he lanced it and marked him for evacuation to the Casualty Clearing Station at Corbie. At Corbie, the Medical Officer marked Venables for the next train to a Base Hospital.

The next day, a spotlessly clean ambulance train stood in the railway siding adjoining the Clearing Station. All morning the Orderlies had been busily loading up the stretcher cases and when the last few were being carried in, a party of forty men, Venables among them, walked and limped alongside.

The journey to Rouen only took a few hours. When the train stopped in the siding, a fleet of motor ambulances arrived alongside and sped quickly into the night carrying their load of broken humanity to various hospitals.

Venables with others went to No. 5 General Hospital. After a hot bath and change of clothes, Venables was shown his bed. It had a spring mattress! Blankets! Sheets and pillows! The luxury of comfort and cleanliness made him forget the hardship of the past. Venables dropped quickly into a sleep of peace and security.

4. Rain and Snow: Mud and Frost

The Sister in charge of the marquee was a regular nurse of uncertain years, much burdened with her responsibilities; she was assisted by a jolly member of the VAD (Voluntary Aid Detachment). They came around in the early morning making beds and preparing for the MO (Medical Officer), but as Venables was a new arrival he was permitted to sleep until just before the MO arrived. The MO examined his foot and said, "That's a nasty foot deserving Blighty.[11] Today's boat is full isn't it, Sister?" The Sister replied that it was, but there was another boat in three days' time. Venables could have jumped out of bed with excitement.

There was a Grenadier in the bed opposite to him with water on the knee. When the MO examined him he said, "A little rest will soon put you right." After lights out the Grenadier took off his bandage, ran up and down the ward and then flogged his knee with a wet towel until he could hardly bear the pain. Other men resorted to similar devices and repeated the dose several times during the night, to get just a little worse than they were in order to be sent home. Two days later the MO was again making his round and marking for Blighty. Venables was excited, though not quite so confident as his foot was better.

"Um. You're better too quickly my boy. I can't send you," said the MO.

When he came to the Grenadier he said, "This man is not improving, we had better send him home." When

---

11 An informal reference to Great Britain.

the MO had gone the Grenadier said to the disappointed Venables:

"You young fool! Why didn't you take the bandage off and put your foot out in the cold for an hour or two as I told you?"

After Christmas, Venables was moved to No. 2 Convalescent Camp, Rouen. This was the first step back to the Line and the gradual shedding of various comforts.

Billiard Room in the No. 2 Convalescent Camp
YMCA hut at Rouen, 18th May 1917.
© IWM Q 005452.

The mattresses and sheets of the hospital were left behind. In their place, he had an ordinary straw bed and blankets. He wore khaki instead of hospital blues. The food, which was served in large dining halls, was good but insufficient and the weekly pay of five francs was exhausted by two suppers at the canteen. His parcels from home discontinued when he went to hospital and had not been resumed. However, he found two men from his home town, who had been in his father's Bible class. They were in the Officers' Mess kitchen and supplied him with a few extras that prevented his getting too hungry.

The first few months of active service had taken most of the joy out of life, and while his faith was still in the Lord Jesus, he was developing some of the cynical fatalism that was common to most men on active service. However, in the centre of the camp there was a large Soldiers' Christian Association Hut with good fires in the reading and writing rooms. Here he came in touch with a similar influence found in the Soldiers' Home at Windsor. The gospel was preached with the same clearness and direct personal appeal and the fresh contact with evangelical Christians did much to restore his spirit and revive his faith.

In the middle of January, he moved to the base camp at Harfleur. The camp had proved hateful in September sunshine, but during the rigours of a severe winter it was infinitely worse. Twelve men shared a bell tent sleeping on a wooden floor with three blankets each. The frost was severe, and the ground was covered with six inches of snow. Each morning they woke with thick hoarfrost on their blankets and with splitting headaches due to lack of air in the closed tent.

The water supply in the wash house was frozen hard and only one tap was kept running. Reveille was at half past six and all other ranks had to wash and shave in the water from the tap, in open sheds, before breakfast. Their supply of water froze in the bowl before they had finished shaving. At 7am they paraded for Sergeant Major's inspection and roll call and were critically examined by the aid of hurricane lamps, as they stood like frozen statues on the parade ground.

The tables in the dining hall had been wiped down the previous night and half a round of bread and one slice of bully beef put for each man's breakfast. The bread and beef froze like a rock to the table during the night and had to be thawed with a mug of very weak tea, whose only virtue was its heat. After breakfast they either marched to the docks to load trains for the front or went a short route march in the snow. Dinner consisted of a very thin bully beef stew and those who were lucky sometimes found half a potato in it.

The YMCA huts and other recreation rooms were overcrowded every night and long queues of men formed up outside in the biting east wind to get a cup of Horlicks malted milk or cocoa. Only one cup was served per man when he arrived at the counter. It often took two hours to get two cups per night, after which it was time to return to the tents for lights out.

In time, Venables was ordered to proceed up the Line to join his Battalion. It wasn't all bad; parcels from home would be renewed and wood to make a fire could be obtained. At Harfleur, there was nothing but red tape and starvation for all but the Officers, NCOs and the base staff.

The party of thirty men and an Officer arrived at the railhead and commenced the eight mile march to Maurepas to join the 3rd Battalion Coldstream Guards. The journey up the Line resembled the previous one except for the cold and wet. The half-starved men laden like pack mules could hardly drag themselves along the muddy road and several fell out on the way. Venables set his teeth and prayed for strength, as he felt himself getting weaker with every step, on what seemed a never-ending march of misery.

They arrived at last opposite a row of Nissen huts and halted at the Orderly Room. As they stood at ease waiting to be posted to their Companies Venables reeled and fell full length in the mud in a dead faint. As he fainted, he heard the voice of the Company Sergeant Major saying, "My poor bloody Regiment. What the hell do they send us men like this for? Some of them fall out on a few miles march, some faint when they get here. What will they be like in the Line? My poor bloody Regiment!"

When he opened his eyes, Venables saw Martin Stevens' smiling face bending over him and his familiar voice brought new life to him. "Hello Ven, don't worry old man you're coming around all right. Come along with me I've got a brew of tea."

Martin Stevens had joined the Battalion during Venables' absence and had been made a stretcher-bearer. Venables followed him to a Nissen hut with rows of men sitting on their kit on either side and with a big fire blazing in the middle. As he entered, he was greeted by Sibson, who had joined the Battalion with Stevens and had just received a parcel from home.

Venables drank the hot tea Stevens had made and ate the brown bread and butter from Sibson's parcel. For supper they all shared a large dixie[12] of porridge made from a packet of Quaker Oats, sweetened and flavoured with Café au Lait. After supper he rolled himself in his

---

12 A cooking pot.

blankets and slept as he had not slept since he left the Convalescent Camp.

The 3rd Coldstream moved for a fortnight's rest and training at the end of February to Billon Camp. Soon after they arrived the frost returned and converted the mud into hard ground and froze all the water solid. The water carts only brought enough for the cooks, so Stevens, Sibson and Venables made nightly trips with petrol tins to the nearest supply about two miles away. On their return they made tea and porridge for supper and saved enough water for washing in the morning. The first morning the Corporal found Venables' water and before Venables was up, the Corporal and a dozen others had washed in it leaving only a tin of thick mud. The next night Venables used his petrol tin of water for a pillow and was able to wash in clean cold water and shave in the remains of his warm breakfast tea.

Billon Camp was near a railhead and ammunition dump, which a German plane bombed, blowing up the ammunition and burning the stores. The Battalion was sent to fill sandbags to build around the ammunition so that the damage from future bombs would be localised. As they were filling the sandbags a coal train drew up.

"I'll be back in ten minutes Sergeant," said the Officer in charge. "Remember the Officers' Mess is short of coal," and he disappeared.

Very quickly, sandbags were filled with coal. A plan was hatched to navigate round the guards at the dump. Later, each man arrived back at camp with his prize. Soon, a dozen open coal fires were smoking down the centre of various huts. However, it began to snow heavily and the holes in the roofs which let the smoke out, also let snow in. The earth floor of the huts became a series of small ponds and a hasty re-arrangement of blankets and ground sheets had to be made on the dry and higher places, round the ponds. The thick black smoke made it impossible to stand up or to see anything more than three feet from the floor. Everything, including faces, was blackened with soot.

The Battalion moved back into the Line and Venables was made a runner attached to No. 1 Company Headquarters at Haie Wood quarry. The petrol tin water was strongly flavoured with petrol, so they were drawing water from the cleanest shell hole they could find, boiling it well before making the tea. Venables went to the shell hole one sunny March morning to fill the dixies for breakfast tea; as he stooped down over the water the rays of the sun revealed the head and shoulders of a dead Frenchman sticking out of the mud at the bottom. He drew water from the next shell hole after giving it a careful examination.

The enemy was preparing to retire to the Hindenburg Line.[13] For several nights the sky behind enemy lines was lit by scores of burning villages. The Germans had evacuated a trench on the east of Saillyisel, and at night the 3rd Battalion moved forward to occupy it. They skirted the remains of the village in drenching rain and entered an

---

13 The Hindenburg Line was a German defensive line on the Western Front in World War One. It was about ninety miles long and stretched between Arras and Laffaux. The Line contained a German Garrison of twenty Divisions every four and a half miles along its length.

old German trench that was a foot deep in mud and water and without dugouts.

Venables began to search in the darkness for something dry to sit on. He was successful in finding a stump sticking out of the side of a trench and wrapping himself in top coat and ground sheet settled down to doze to the sound of pelting rain. The darkness of the night was disturbed only by enemy flares, a few long range shells screeching overhead and the occasional burst of an isolated machine gun.

At stand-to, rum was issued to cold and soaked men and though Venables disliked it, he was so thoroughly starved that he forced himself to drink it. As the day broke, he discovered that he had spent the night on the feet of a German who had been buried face downwards with his feet and boots sticking out into the trench.

At mid-day they were ordered to move back to some dugouts. Sitting on a heap of ruins, Venables could see the three hundred yards of trench where his Company was billeted. Amid the silence and desolation, he thought of the kindness he received from the toughest of the men—the evidence of the image of God in all. Yet it was a likeness sadly marred by the effects of sin.

Suddenly, his thoughts were interrupted as he saw a Company of Irish Guards who were about to cross the other end of the trench. When they saw the Coldstream Guards' unattended kit they commenced to scrounge. He hurried to protest but seeing another Company coming towards him, he decided to protect his own Platoon. When the men returned from fatigue, they reported loss of kit and iron rations and Venables appeared before the Captain charged with neglect of duty while on active service. Despite his protest that one Englishman could not keep two hundred hungry Irishmen from food, Venables was awarded three days 'Confined to Barracks' to be worked off when they returned to proper billets.

During the remainder of March and April the Guards were employed digging railway cuttings and building embankments, so that the Royal Engineers could lay a rail track across the country evacuated by the Germans. The Germans had destroyed all bridges and blown up the roads and railways; the few remaining buildings had been mined with time fuses.

Rations improved with the weather. Rabbits arrived from Australia and mutton from New Zealand; potatoes and bread became more plentiful. Venables worked on an embankment between two colliers throwing the soil from one to the other and although arms and back ached after a long day's work he was able to stick the pace. Hard work, good food and the Spring weather made him a new man; fit for anything.

At the end of April, he was transferred to the Company Signallers, so instead of going with the working parties he was set on signal schemes, like those he had taken part in when he was in England. One station was near Douage Wood where the road from Maurepas drops down to Combles.

A dozen wooden crosses, or broken rifles with pieces of ammunition boxes nailed on to them, marked the graves of Frenchmen. Between the marked graves a man's shoulder or another's feet sticking out of the dried mud revealed the graves of others. Nearly every shell hole, now losing its water in the warm sun, contained the decaying remains of a soldier killed six months before.

On May 20th they marched from Rocquilgny, a village destroyed by the Germans on their retirement, to Billon Farm Camp crossing the whole of the Somme battle ground. The route took them through Les Boeufs and Ginchy along the sunken road that had been the scene of the Guards' attacks in September. Those who took part in the action noted the various landmarks and spoke of places where comrades fell. Apart from this they marched in silence and safety, where they had once experienced the din of exploding shells, the rattle of machine guns and the cry of men as they either killed or were killed. It was a broken and desolate landscape, to which no animal or bird life had yet ventured to return. Weeds shrouded the sleep of countless dead.

The following day they moved on to the village of Vaux sur Somme; as they marched, the landscape changed from death to life and a load seemed to lift from their minds. The birds sang, the spring flowers bloomed, the long rows of poplars by the roadside were unspoilt by shellfire. Peasants worked in green luxurious fields and all nature rejoiced in the warm spring sunshine.

They were billeted in a spacious hay barn and in the evenings, coffee and omelettes prepared by Madame, were enjoyed in a clean farm kitchen. A saint entering Heaven could not experience a greater thrill than they, as they marched from the abode of death and destruction to the unspoilt beauties of nature in springtime.

5. The Battle of Passchendaele

After a short rest the Coldstream Guards journeyed by train through Calais and St. Omer, then marched to the hamlet of Clairmareis, behind the Ypres salient. Good billets, sports and training were their happy lot for a fortnight. Venables was selected from the Company Signallers to go to Divisional Headquarters for a course of instruction on the Power Buzzer and Amplifier, which were an underground wireless transmitter and receiver.

Assault on Passchendaele 12th October – 6th November 1917: A soldier running along a corduroy track through Chateau Wood. Originally captioned 'The Way to the Front', probably posed. © IWM E AUS 001233.

On completion of his course, Venables was posted to the Permanent Staff of Battalion Headquarters Signals and had to settle in with the following old soldiers: Chick, a gamekeeper from Norfolk; Harry, a gentleman from Bath; Robo, an iron-founder from Sheffield; Dusty, a fisherman from Bolton; Patch, a cheap jeweller from Birmingham; Sarpy, a collier from Warwickshire; and Venables himself, a Bible puncher from Staffordshire.

Chick and Harry were Linesmen responsible for running out and maintaining the telephone wires when broken by shellfire. Though continually in danger, Chick had been with the Battalion from the beginning of the war. The remainder were Telephone Operators, and all had been home, wounded and had returned to France for the second time. Venables belonged to the strange type who went to voluntary Church Parade, did not smoke, drink or swear and was sometimes seen reading his Bible. At first the old soldiers treated him with considerable suspicion, which he quickly lived down, until he was eventually accepted by them all.

The Guards had been out of the Line for the record period of three months and they were fully aware that this could not continue much longer. At last it was revealed there was to be a determined effort to clear the Belgian coast of the enemy, capturing his submarine bases and the aeroplane hangars from which he bombed London. The fields round the villages were set out to represent the enemy positions and his trenches; concrete pill boxes and strong points were marked by full scale models made from aerial photographs. The positions were explained to all ranks and were stormed several times a day in field exercises, until every man became familiar with them.

*Gotha G.IV heavy bombers of the England Squadron
(Kagohl 3 or "England Geschwader") lined-up for take-off
from Nieuwmunster, near Ostend on the Belgian coast, were
the first bombers despatched to Flanders for the daylight
raids on London in the spring 1917. Note the distinctive crew
markings on the bombers and the crashed aircraft in the
distance. © IWM Q 073552 A.*

On the 29th June the 3rd Coldstream prepared to relieve
the 3rd Grenadiers. The way to the Front Line through
well-kept communication trenches made easy going
despite heavy rain. Venables and a companion Signaller
quickly found the dugout in the Front Line, where they
took charge of a Power Buzzer. The other fellow took first
turn on duty and Venables, though wet through to the
skin, was soon fast asleep, waking up two hours later to
do duty.

When breakfast time came, they discovered that the
rain had played havoc with their rations stored in a
sandbag. The bread and biscuits were soaked. The bacon
was covered with tea and two tins of bully had pounded
the whole lot together with wet sticky sugar.

They scraped the tea off the bacon, with as little fat,
sandbag and bread as possible and made an excellent brew;
then, having carefully dried the bread in the sun and fried
the sweetened bacon, they made a good breakfast.

On the 26th July the 3rd Coldstream went into the Line with Battalion Headquarters at Chasseur Farm in the ruins of Boesinghe. Their dugouts were built of sandbags in the ruins of the farm buildings and were covered with heaps of debris. They were good splinter-proof shacks, but a direct hit by a shell would have blown them and their occupants sky high and they were constantly under shellfire.

One afternoon Venables and a man named Turvey were sitting outside the Signallers' dugout making tea in a petrol tin on a fire, which they carefully tended to avoid smoke. "It's boiling, Venables. Fetch the tea," said Turvey.

As Venables turned and took two steps towards the dugout, a shell rushed over the top of the dugout and exploded on the fire. Venables was flung on his face and

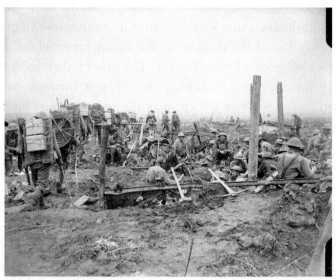

Battle of Pilckem Ridge. Scene on captured ground near Hooge. British troops digging trenches, a fatigue party wearing Yukon packs going up and wounded being brought down. 31st July 1917. © IWM Q 005721.

covered with a shower of dirt and stones, as Turvey fell back with a large piece of shell in his stomach.

The stretcher-bearers carried Turvey to the field dressing station where he died in a few hours. Venables stood in the dugout and felt himself all over, but he was only suffering from bruises and shock, so he sat down to collect himself. "What about that tea Ven?" said Chick. "Let's try again." So, they made another refreshing brew that steadied all their nerves.

Early on the following morning a young officer from Eton and an old soldier, making a fine combination of courage, crossed the canal and found the enemy's position very lightly held. It was resolved to cross the canal in force at once and establish a position on the high ground beyond. The Signallers were kept busy transmitting orders to various sections and early in the afternoon a message came for the machine gun Officer; this was Venables' responsibility. He set off for the Front Line in the terrific heat, unthinkingly leaving his rifle behind. (No one was allowed in the Front unarmed.) As he left the communication trench and turned down the canal bank, he found the men were preparing to cross the bed of the empty canal and attack the enemy.

"Where's the machine gun Officer?" Venables asked.

"Further up," came the reply.

Venables went around two traverses of trench and walked into the Adjutant who asked, "What are you doing here, Signaller?"

"A message for the machine gun Officer, Sir" he replied.

"Let me see it … all right. Get a telephone and connect to Headquarters from here at once."

Venables found a telephone at one of the Company Signal Posts and in a short time selected the right wire and got through to Battalion Headquarters. In the meantime, the guns put down a barrage and the men crossed the canal and climbed up the opposite bank.

"Through to Headquarters Sir," shouted Venables above the din.

"I'll speak to the Colonel," replied the Adjutant as he sat on the bank with Venables beside him.

A red rocket shot up into the air out of the smoke of the barrage. It hung for a few seconds and then fell. Others followed it in quick succession. The rockets were the enemy's SOS to their own gunners and the din suddenly increased as the enemy replied to the attack.

"Venables! A rifle, quick!" called the Adjutant as a dozen Germans left a dugout and were running away not a hundred yards off. Venables jumped into the trench but all the rifles had gone over the top with the men.

The Adjutant swore and shouted, "Get Headquarters again." But the telephone wire had been broken by the German bombardment. "The line's disconnected Sir."

"Go back to Headquarters at once," ordered the Adjutant.

"Sir," replied Venables, and his heart sank, for Headquarters was the other side of the barrage. He made his way as slowly as possible along the trench to the place where the communication trench turned off the Front Line. Here, Royal Engineers crouched in a corner to miss the flying splinters.

"Where the bloody hell are you going? Stop here you damned fool. You can't get through that," they shouted.

After a moment's indecision he was suddenly lifted off his feet and hurled forward, into the inferno of bursting shells and his only course was to duck and run.

He stumbled through the ruins of the communication trench. A continual shower of stones and dirt fell on his tin hat. Several times he was blown flat by exploding shells, while others seemed to whistle past his ears. The smell of high explosive, which he thought at first was gas, gripped his chest. He could see only a few yards in the smoke and was deafened by the explosions.

After what seemed hours, but must have been minutes, he found himself out in the sun with an earthwork running to his right. A solitary soldier crouched against it.

"Is this the way to Chasseur Farm?" asked Venables. The man grinned as Venables repeated his question and then he grinned again and continued grinning. Venables shuddered and passed on.

The barrage continued on Venables' right, but stray shells burst uncomfortably near as he came to the door of a dugout which housed the Advance Divisional Headquarters.

Venables drew aside the gas blankets and quickly descended thirty steps, arriving at the bottom hot, pale and shaking all over; his tin hat was supported on the short vertical bristles of his hair.

"What's up Ven?" said Chick's familiar voice.

"Go on top and see," replied Venables.

"Some RE Signallers have just made some tea. I'll get you a drop and you'll feel better," replied Chick.

The capture of the canal bank and enemy positions established a bridgehead over the canal, which saved many lives. Though the enemy counter-attacked he failed to regain the lost ground. As Venables reflected, he realised how God had answered his prayer not to take life. With the enemy running he could not find a rifle. Under enemy bombardments, God had preserved him, unharmed. As he thought about the war, he quietly dropped off to sleep with a very thankful heart.

British infantry crossing the bridge over the Yser canal at Boezinge, 5th August 1917. This bridge was constructed by the Royal Engineers after the British advance had passed the canal. © IWM Q 002681.

At the end of August, the 3rd Battalion moved forward to Charterhouse Camp by the ruins of Emile Farm near Boesinghe and Elverdinghe. It was constantly shelled and bombed so the camouflaged tents were scattered over a wide area; the inside of each tent was dug out to a depth of eighteen inches and surrounded by a wall of sandbags filled with soil as a precaution against flying splinters from shells.

While the precaution had been taken to scatter the tents, four company cookers stood in a row, wheel to wheel in the centre of the camp. One morning, the cookhouse sounded for dinner and the cooks stood by their equipment putting final touches to the stew, while orderlies crowded round waiting to carry the appetising mixture to hungry troops.

A large shell dropped on the middle cooker, smashing them all to pieces and blowing stew, cooks and orderlies all over the camp. There was no dinner that day. Fifteen men were killed or wounded.

One Sunday afternoon the Nonconformist Chaplain arrived to conduct a voluntary service. He collected about a dozen men and two Officers, with a couple of drummers to lead the singing.

As the service began the shelling suddenly intensified and detracted from the spiritual side of the Padre's message. He hurried through the service and commenced the closing prayer. A large shell dropped a few yards to the right. The congregation ducked as dirt and stones came down in showers. The Chaplain said a loud "Amen" as another shell dropped on the Officers' Mess a few yards away and the service closed abruptly as all ran for cover.

The weather continued to be exceptionally wet and the Division occupied the forest area round Proven, doing periods of duty in the Line throughout September. In early October the 3rd Coldstream were in the Proven area training for a further advance and several men joined the Signallers, including Corporal Boxer and a man called Wonky. Boxer was a genial Berkshire Policeman who attended church when at home. Venables and he soon found they had lots in common. Wonky however was a mystery. When a shell dropped, he trembled like a leaf and his eyes stood out like saucers.

A shell bursts within ten yards of the photographer near Zonnebeke during the Battle of Passchendaele, 23rd September 1917. © IWM Q 002890.

It was evening time and while the rest assembled in the wet canteen, Venables and Boxer ate supper together in a tent. They were due back up the Line. A big attack was planned.

"If the worst comes to the worst," said Boxer, "I've always done my best and attended church fairly regularly. A man can't do more."

"It's faith in Christ that saves and makes us sure," said Venables, as they heard the voices of the merrymakers outside. The tent door flapped.

"Whatever has Wonky got to go for, Sergeant?" said one. "He'll frighten us to death before we start."

"Why shouldn't he go as well as the rest of us?" said another, as they all stumbled into the tent.

"Leave him out, Sergeant. We'll do his job. We shall be a thousand times better off without him," said Venables.

"Orders is orders. He's got to go. We shall have to put up with him," said the Sergeant.

Next day they marched to Eton Camp, Elverdinghe, in pouring rain. This kept the enemy's bombing planes away but made the camp a mire. The following day they prepared for the Line and still it rained. They hoped the weather would cause the attack to be cancelled but winter was approaching, and it was necessary to move the waterlogged Front Line to higher ground either by retreat or advance. Going back wasn't on. Attack they must.

Darkness fell quickly and the night was as black as ink. The road through Elversinghe was blocked with traffic, groping its way without lights in pouring rain. Motor lorries, horse-drawn limbers, pack mules, despatch riders and troops of all arms jostled and swore at one another, but the enemy's guns were silent. He appeared to be unaware a 'relief' was taking place. But, as they joined the Langemarck Road a salvo of shells burst on the head of the relief. When the Signallers reached the place where the shells had dropped it was all in confusion.

The hard road was pitted with shell holes, shattered tree trunks were lying across them and stretcher-bearers groped about for the wounded, guided only by their groans. The men moving out of the Line were urging each other to get a move on, while the stretcher-bearers shouted to them to go carefully. Someone trod on a wounded man whose shriek rent the air and the Officers urged them to make less noise, as the enemy's listening posts were close to.

The Sergeant called out, "Battalion Headquarters this way." Venables followed the voice and jumped into a trench behind the pillbox at Martins Mill. The others followed, including Wonky who shook like a leaf and was dumb with fear. The shells kept dropping round the pillbox as they crouched in the trench and the pillbox rocked in the mud. Suddenly, Wonky jumped out of the trench and disappeared into the darkness....

The 2nd Battalion Coldstream Guards was to attack first. When it had gained its objectives the 3rd would pass through and take the final objective.

Headquarters left Martins Hill in the early hours of the morning and joined the rest of the Battalion behind the low earthworks on the ruins of Cannes Farm. The rain and shelling ceased and an hour before dawn there was a stillness that could be felt.

Column of German prisoners of war, captured during the Battle of Langemarck, being marched into captivity. Photograph taken near Proven. Note a British hospital train in the background. © IWM Q 003942.

As the first streak of grey was showing itself in the clouds, rum was issued and bayonets fixed. As it brightened into dawn a big naval gun boomed behind the line and the shell rolled lazily overhead and burst some miles behind the enemy Line.

Immediately the whole concourse of heavy and field artillery, trench mortars and machine guns joined in a thunderous roar. The flashes of guns danced against the dull grey sky and reflected in the sea of shell holes. Every bush and fold in the land spat flame and death, phosphorous and iron, on the enemy's line.

Ten minutes later the barrage moved forward with mathematical precision and the 2nd Battalion rose from its position, crossed the stream waist deep in water and followed it.

Several red rockets shot up into the air out of the smoke and the Signallers crouched nearer their earthwork as the German barrage burst all round them. They could hardly hear one another speak, as an Officer stood, watch in hand and called out above the din.

"Five minutes to go."

"Three minutes to go."

"One minute to go."

"Half a minute to go."

"Lead on."

As Headquarters moved forward about a hundred yards behind the Advance Company and crossed the stream to reach higher ground, it left the enemy's counter-barrage behind. Venables could see the British barrage some distance in front sweeping everything before it.

Buildings fell in clouds of dust and trees were uprooted and shattered to pieces. It seemed impossible for anything to live in such an inferno, but when it had passed over the enemy strong-points, their machine guns took a deadly toll on the advancing infantry.

A German plane flew low over the shell holes and reported the positions to the guns somewhere in the Houthulst Forest. The enemy's guns opened with deadly accuracy. The plane returned and swooping down, opened fire with its machine-gun and afterwards returned to direct the gunfire. A large shell dropped into the shell hole next to Venables and three men came tumbling out saying,

"Boxer's dead, got a lump in his chest."

Headquarters was moving again, and this action relieved the nerves of Venables and those with him. The final objective had been gained and the men were digging for their lives a short distance in front. The Signallers had found the position of the Companies and commenced to run out telephone wires to them when their contact aeroplane appeared overhead. It was a biplane recognised by two long streamers that flew from its wings and the call of its horn in Morse: "RU RU RU", as it tried to identify the men who were digging.

"Where's the aeroplane sheet Venables?" said the Sergeant.

"Boxer had it," replied Venables.

"Go back and fetch it quick."

Retracing his steps, Venables found the aeroplane sheet near to Boxer's body and was glad he lay face down. As Venables made his way back, he saw a Chaplain holding a cross before the eyes of the dying man as he prayed with him.

The Sergeant and Venables pegged the sheet to the ground and began to call the aeroplane. The pilot saw it and asked on his horn: "RU RU (Who are you?).

"GCC GCC (3rd Coldstream Guards)," they replied. "All objectives gained."

"OK", came the reply from the plane as it turned and disappeared to the rear.

On the 18th October the 3rd Coldstream arrived for rest and training in the French village of Herleulingham, behind St. Omer. Venables' first task was to write to the relatives of those who had fallen in the last action, as letters from the Front usually carried the sad news before the official information arrived.

First Battle of Passchendaele. Guardsmen, including men of the 4th Battalion, Coldstream Guards, with a telescope and Lewis Gun resting on wooden post about to open fire on a German aeroplane, near Langemarck (Langemark-Poelkapelle), 12th October 1917. © IWM Q 003012.

During this period, Venables learned that his old school friend Will Hazlewood was wounded and missing. Then he heard that Charlie Mawson of the Household Battalion had been killed. Mawson had attended the Soldiers' Home at Windsor after Venables had left and was well known to Stevens. All three had met and prayed together the night before Mawson was killed.

The summer was over, and the end of the war was as far off as ever. The offensive had not yielded the expected result owing to the weather, which always appeared to favour the enemy. News came that Russia had made peace with Germany, releasing all Germany's Eastern Armies for the Western Front. This was followed by the Italian collapse and the despatch of a British and French Army Corps to Italy. The future was far from bright, but the Private Soldier lived only for the present and Venables was due for leave.

Wonky had been found wandering about in the back area and sent to Herleulingham to be Court-Martialled. His defence was that he was shell-shocked and as Venables was the last to see him he had to give evidence.

He was marched before an imposing array of Officers and was asked, "How near did the shells drop on the Langemarck Road on the night of October 8th?"

Venables was about to reply that he had not taken a tape measure with him and even if he had done so, he could not have used it as it was dark, but he remembered he was due for leave.

"I don't know Sir."

"Did they drop within fifty, twenty, or ten yards?

"Within ten yards sir."

All he did know was they were near enough to kill some and put the wind up the remainder. Wonky was sentenced to ten years penal servitude.

It had been a difficult time. Death stalked them all, the weather chided and food was often in short supply. So, Venables was relieved when one day the Orderly Corporal announced:

"16236 Guardsman Venables, parade at 7.30am at the Orderly Room to proceed on fourteen days leave, to England."

6. The Battle of Cambrai

It is impossible to describe the feelings of an infantryman returning home after fourteen months' active service. Venables and one other man from his Battalion seemed to walk on air as they hurried to catch the train to Calais and sail the next day for Dover. Anxious eyes gazed into the November mist as the boat ploughed her way home. Two Naval Destroyers dashed by, attracting attention for a short time, and when they looked again, they saw the outline of the cliffs at Dover. The white cliffs of England always thrill her returning sons, but for those returning from the Battlefields of Flanders there was something deeper; there was a strange combination of thankfulness for their own good fortune and the haunting memory of those who would never return.

At Victoria Train Station, they were met by a company of elderly gentlemen, who piloted them across London to the Regimental Pay Office and then to Euston. They walked proudly down Regent Street in full fighting kit, their worn and shabby uniforms made to look as smart as possible. In the crowded night train from Euston a seat was willingly found for men from the Front and they began to realise that they were persons and not numbers.

Arriving home, Venables opened the latch of the back door and walked in. His sisters and mother busied themselves with a hot meal while his father talked. After family prayers he had a hot bath and went to bed. His mother kissed him as she tucked him up and said good night. Venables tried to pray, but thoughts confused and strange hurried his mind and as he snuggled down in spotlessly white sheets, it seemed like a beautiful dream. He dropped off into a deep, deep sleep.

The fourteen days' leave passed quickly away and the break with home and friends was made the second time. When Venables arrived at Victoria Station between five and six o'clock in the morning, it was crowded with men from all parts of the British Isles, who had arrived in London on night trains. They filled the coffee bar for their last meal in England, slept on the seats or on the station floor under greatcoats, while a few chatted to friends who were seeing them off.

As soon as the barrier was opened the Military Police woke the sleepers and interrupted the final farewells with, "Time to get on the train mate." A big highlander lay asleep on the platform. A Policeman shook his shoulder. He jumped up, swore, rubbed his eyes and then as one waking from a dream, grunted and joined the stream of men making for the trains.

(The author) Guardsman George Venables at the end of fourteen days' leave after the Battles of the Somme and Passchendaele. Returning to the Battle of Cambrai (Gouzeaucourt) December 1917. © Venables Family.

The whistle blew, the train drew out of the station and they were on their way again. Venables was in a compartment filled with infantry and gunners, who were fully aware of what awaited them. There was a sullen tense silence, which a gunner broke by saying:

"This morning's paper says there's a big push at Cambrai and the Cavalry's got through."

"Heard about Cavalry before," grunted an infantryman.

"It's something more than usual. They say they are ringing the bells today."

"Tolling them you mean," said another.

A few hours before, each man had been the hero and centre of a loving circle, now he was just a number moving on to hardship, danger and perhaps mutilation or death.

Tank F4 at the Tank Driving School during the special training for the Battle of Cambrai at Wailly, 21st October 1917. Over 400 tanks were gathered for that training. © IWM Q 006297.

At Calais they learned the Guards had moved and were engaged in fierce fighting round Cambrai.

After three days they trained to Bapaume, where they spent the night in the ruins. The next day Venables and a companion continued their journey by hitch-hiking through the desolate Somme country to find the Battalion in the ruins of Metz. He received a warm welcome from the Signallers, who told him about the battle, the way the 1st Battalion had been cut up at Bourlon Wood, the success of the tanks and that the Division was about to move out of the Line.

He found Stevens before dark and as rations were very short, they set out together to find a canteen. After a fruitless search he returned tired and hungry to his billet, which was an open shed with three tiers of beds made by a wooden frame with wire netting stretched over it. Venables crawled into bed with a man below him and one on either side. Then he fell asleep.

Whoof! Whoof! He woke and lifted himself on his elbows. The roar of the guns rocked the shed and an occasional shell was falling near.

"He's shelling the cross-roads. It's far enough from here," said the next man reassuringly.

The guns still roared as the bugle sounded reveille.

After a breakfast of two slices of bully beef and three biscuits, blankets were rolled in bundles and kits packed ready to commence the march to the Back Area. As the morning advanced the roar of the guns died down and rumours were circulated that the Germans had broken the Line. This was confirmed by an order to hand their packs to the transport, draw extra ammunition and all available rations and stand by, in fighting order.

The Germans had captured the last line of British guns and were moving up their own to fresh positions, so there was no gunfire. The Brigade went into artillery formation and advanced towards the ridge. Reaching the ridge the enemy opened sharp rifle and machine gun fire forcing the Platoons into extended order. In this way, the men went straight at the enemy in short rushes.

A few Officers had collected all the odd men they could in a trench, just beyond the ridge and held the enemy's advance. As the Guards attacked and passed through them, the watchers rose and gave a mighty British cheer. The machine guns and rifles rattled away, and the air was full of whistling bullets that sent up little spurts of dust as they hit the ground all round.

Battalion Headquarters halted for a few moments in a sunken road where the Medical Officer had established his Advance Aid Post. The stretcher cases were being carried to a motor ambulance on the main road and those with only a short time to live were made as comfortable as possible in a tin shed.

Stevens and his mate put a man down by Venables as they went inside the shed to make a comfortable place for him. He looked up and asked for a drink. Venables moistened his lips from his water bottle and the man murmured, "I'm done chum." Several Bible texts crowded Venables' mind but he was interrupted. "Lead on Signallers!" ordered the Sergeant and Venables went into battle, thankful the man was in Stevens' good hands.

They reached the place where hand to hand fighting had taken place and hurried by a group of dead bodies, half in khaki and half in field grey. The ruins of Gouzeaucourt were recaptured and the Brigade dug in for the night on the other side of the village. Battalion Headquarters occupied the dugout, under a battery of six-inch howitzers, which was full of gunners' kit. It was all new and evidently belonging to men just out from England. Despite protests from Venables and others, they proceeded to find what was worth finding. When all the kit was in a heap on the floor the gunners' voices were heard outside and one of them came in.

"What do you want in here?" said a Signaller.

"We want our kit," replied a very youthful soldier.

"This yours?" the Signaller asked, pointing to a heap on the floor. "Fritz has been in while you were away and pinched what's any good. You're lucky to find anything after running away and leaving it."

The gunners began to sort their kit as the Coldstream men sat around. Whether they thought it was Fritz or not, Venables did not know, but they were wise enough not to suggest that the Coldstream Guards had been scrounging.

"Poor little beggars," said Chick when they had gone on top to the guns. "Looks as though they have only just left school."

The attack was resumed at daybreak supported by tanks. A party of Signallers, including Venables, took up a position on the outskirts of the village on the road from Fins, in some slit trenches dug by the Front Line the night before. The position commanded a view of the valley and ridge opposite, which was the Brigade's objective. The Signallers ran a telephone wire back to Battalion Headquarters and tried to get in touch with the Front Companies with electric lamps.

Two Signallers were in one hole about six feet long and four feet deep, with a telephone connected back to Headquarters. Two were in another with an electric lamp and Venables was in a third with eyes just above the ground watching the advancing troops and looking out for their electric lamp signals.

The enemy spotted the newly dug ground and, suspecting that it was held by reserves, commenced to shell heavily. The telephone was smashed and the two men, wounded by splinters, quickly disappeared towards the rear.

A few minutes later another shell blew in the next hole and buried the occupants up to their shoulders. Venables jumped out of his trench and with his trenching tool freed their arms, then they worked quickly, with shells bursting all round them, until they were all released.

They made for another hole, scanned the ridge for lamp signals from the Front Line, but without results. As all their kit was smashed, they decided to return to Headquarters for instructions. They were relieved the next night and went into dugouts between Metz and Gouzeaucourt.

Two days later the 3rd Coldstream returned to the Line on a bright frosty moonlight night. They followed the road on the left of the village and down a narrow track to the station ruins. As they passed down the track the enemy artillery opened fire and they fell on their faces as the shells screeched and crashed all around them.

"Lead! Lead on!" shouted the Sergeant. They dashed along leaving dead and wounded where they lay.

Battalion Headquarter Officers were in a dugout down thirty steps and the Signallers in a splinter-proof shack covered with sandbags in a railway cutting near the station.

The telephone exchange was already fixed up with wires to the Front Companies and to Brigade Headquarters in the rear.

Venables was on duty in the early hours of the morning when the enemy suddenly began to shell. The shells slid over the roof of the dugout and burst on the railway a few yards away. The candles flickered on the dugout side with each explosion and the men woke and sat with their backs to the earth side of the dugout, smoking cigarettes. Venables rang round all the Companies and Brigade Headquarters but could not get a reply from any.

"All the wires are gone, Chick," he said.

"They'll remain gone until it stops," replied Chick.

The shack rocked with each explosion and the noise was deafening. Suddenly the bank behind their backs heaved, the candles all went out and the whole place seemed to be falling in. Venables, who was nearest the door, rolled out and ran down the steps of the Officers' dugout. He sat half way down trembling like a leaf and then, thoroughly ashamed of himself, crawled back. The candles and cigarettes were reignited; the others sat in the same places as before.

"Breeze up, Ven?" asked Chick. Come on, it's quieter now, let's put the wires right." In less than half an hour communication was restored with all companies.

The Division was relieved and the 3rd Coldstream arrived back at Gouzeaucourt on the bitterly cold night of December 5th. All they had for a bed was the ground and bivouac sheet. The Signallers made a fire, but just as it was blazing up an enemy plane droned overhead and the fire was promptly put out. They all lay in a row on the bivouac sheet and slept, waking a long time before dawn frozen and stiff. The long march to Etricourt restored their circulation and they entrained for the Back Area.

7. Winter in Arras

The remainder of December was spent in training in the village of Bernville behind Arras, where their billet was an old inn and their bed a stone floor. The frost was severe, the snow was deep and there was very little fuel, but the casualties at Gouzeaucourt made blankets plentiful. So, when they were not drilling, walking, or playing football, they sat on the stone floor wrapped in blankets.

A soldier walking through the snow. Cambrai front, 22nd December 1917. © IWM Q 010599.

The Divisional Nonconformist Chaplain obtained the use of a tin shed ten feet square for services. He put a brazier in the middle with a good coal fire, but the tins that formed the sides were a foot off the floor and the roof was six inches above the sides. This meant that their feet and heads were in a biting east wind while their middles were baked in front and frozen behind. Ten to a dozen men went to the services. They were helpful times and all who attended were conscious of the Lord Jesus's presence and blessing.

On January 2nd they marched into Arras and were billeted in the College Communals. Chick and Harry had gone on in advance to take over the billet and, having an hour or two to spare, they 'found' a heap of straw and half a dozen large bags of coal, which they hid under the straw in a corner of the classroom. When the others came in wet, tired and cold, they had no wood to start a fire.

"What about the blackboard?" said Robo.

"It's on an inventory. The Quarterbloke has taken it over from a Froggy and signed for it," said Chick.

"We shall have to have some sticks from somewhere" replied Robo. Venables was placed as sentry at the door and in a few minutes the blackboard was reduced to a heap of sticks with trenching tools and bayonets. They had just started a fire and served up tea when the Colonel walked in.

"Tee Hun!" said the old soldier Chick, and they jumped to attention.

"All right, carry on," said the Colonel. "Are you comfortable?"

"Yes Sir," they choroused.

His eyes caught the pile of sticks and a sack of coal.

"Where did you get these from?"

"They were here when we came Sir."

"You know all the furniture is on an inventory and has to be accounted for."

"Yes Sir."

"Goodnight."

"Goodnight Sir."

The Colonel left, having wise eyes but seeing not.

Next morning Venables was sitting at the telephone exchange when the large form of the Sergeant Major entered the doorway and strutting across the room enquired with an equally large voice:

"Signaller! Signaller! What's the time?"

Venables jumped to attention and said "10.20, Sir."

This brief scene struck a humorous vein in Venables. Moving his long, thin body and using his equally thin voice, Venables strutted after the Sergeant Major and said, "Signaller! Signaller! What's the time?"

The Sergeant Major turned around and stood face to face with Venables.

"Are you laughing at me my lad?"

"No Sir," said Venables now rigidly at attention.

"Attend Commanding Officer's orders for laughing at the Sergeant Major."

"Sir." replied Venables.

"You told a lie Ven," said Harry. "Chaps, Ven told a lie."

"Well, it was the best sort," countered Venables. "It did not deceive any of you, not even the Sergeant Major."

The school playground was a large area of asphalt and it made a parade ground after the Sergeant Major's heart. Half an hour later Venables was crossing the playground as Battalion parade was forming up. The drum tapped, calling the parade to attention and all men walking about near the parade, however employed, were also supposed to halt and stand to attention. Venables was about ten yards from the billet door and instead of standing still, he risked it and dived for the door.

"Come here that man," called a familiar voice.

Venables turned about and stood to attention before the Drill Sergeant.

"Why did you not stand still at the tap of the drum?"

Venables really did not know, so he stood rigidly to attention and gazed at the Drill Sergeant.

"What are you looking at me like that for? Attend Commanding Officer's orders for dumb insolence."

"Sir," replied Venables and wondered how the charge would read. He didn't have to wait too long to find out. "Guardsman Venables charged with gross insubordination in that while on active service at 10.20am he laughed at the Sergeant Major and at 11am he looked fiercely at the Drill Sergeant."

Perhaps even the Warrant Officers saw the humour, if humour is part of their make-up, for it was the last he heard of it.

The side of the town near the Line and round the station was a mass of ruins, but the other side had escaped with only a few houses destroyed. A few shops remained open, as well. The Signallers handed half of their pay to Venables, who provided supper from the shops selling French savouries.

One evening after shopping he went to the theatre to hear the string band of the Royal Artillery. It made an enjoyable change, though the theatre was well ventilated with shell holes in the roof and walls. When he returned to the billets he found the others playing halfpenny nap round the fire.

"There's been a chap looking for you; just come up with a draft. He's a Bible puncher and looks as miserable as sin," said Patch. Venables had heard from Windsor that a man named Young, with a serious disposition, had left England and was on the lookout for him. He went to the classroom where Young's section was billeted and found a youth with a very solemn and anxious face. Having introduced himself Young said:

"Isn't this terrible?"

"Terrible?" repeated the surprised Venables. "It's all right here. A good dry billet and plenty of food. I'll take you shopping tomorrow night."

"Up the Line I mean," added Young.

"Oh, that's cushy here, too. The trenches and dugouts are well made and not too much shelling to worry you."

"The war. It's simply awful isn't it?" persisted a frightened voice and pained face.

"Well yes. I suppose it is," said Venables slowly, "but it's no use worrying about that and it's surprising what you can get used to if you make the best of things."

The bugle was sounding the Last Post outside, so Venables said goodnight with a promise to return the next day.

There was a YMCA hut in the centre of the town near the ruins of the Hotel de Ville. In one of the small rooms a few of the Divisional Signallers held a Bible reading and Prayer meeting, which Venables found very helpful. They announced a Breaking of Bread Meeting for the Sunday morning, but he was unable to attend as he was on duty.

When he first went to France Venables did not attend any Communion services, but later, through Stevens' influence, they went together to the Nonconformist services whenever they were held. This was possible two or three times a year and while they were far more formal than anything he had been used to, there was something about them that he never forgot.

About a dozen men met in a YMCA hut, or the corner of a field and knelt together as the Padre presented to each the symbols of Christ,[14] saying:

"This is my body which is given for you."

"This is my blood which is shed for you."

As they remembered their Lord they bowed in simple worship and their souls were strengthened for the battle.

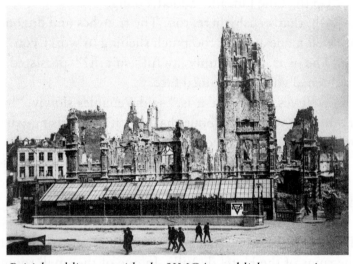

British soldiers outside the YMCA establishment at Arras, 30th June 1917. Note the destroyed belfry and the Town Hall in the background. © IWM Q 078351.

---

14 This is a reference to the bread and wine used in a Communion Service, conducted by a Chaplain.

When they were preparing to leave Arras, they saw the Quartermaster handing over the billets to a French Officer and checking each room with an inventory. The inventory that hung in their classroom had gone the same way as the blackboard. This would put Venables in an awkward position, so the others very thoughtfully suggested that he disappear. This he gladly did and waited out of sight until the Quartermaster and the Frenchman left. He learned that when they asked for the board the Signallers stoutly affirmed it had never been there and though it was unthinkable anybody should believe them, they did not hear any more about it.

The Division took over a portion of the Front north of the river Scarpe. The 3rd Coldstream went into Line near Roeux caves in front of the ruins of Fampoux on the 19th of January. The Battalion spent the next sixteen days digging fresh defences, holding the line and carrying ammunition and rations to the Front. The dugouts were deep and comfortable, the trenches were well made and drained and rations were plentiful.

When in the Front Line there were the usual raids and patrols and there was a considerable amount of shelling with gas and high explosive, but the Signallers had no difficulty in maintaining communications. They returned to Arras on the 26th of January and enjoyed the luxury of a hot bath, a clean change of underclothes and beds consisting of straw and blankets.

All through the winter the Germans were transferring their forces from East to West. The 14th Corps had moved to Italy and the necessary reinforcements had not arrived from home. Everybody knew that they were poorly prepared for the enemy offensive, which was bound to come in the Spring. The hope of speedy victory, which had characterised most men the previous year, was replaced by an anxious foreboding. When it was announced early in February it was necessary to reduce the number of Battalions in a Brigade from four to three and that the three would be expected to do the work of four, the old soldiers despaired.

On the 8th February, a dull wet wintry day, the three Battalions marched out of Arras along the Vimy Road and left the Division. The General Officer Commanding Guards Division and the three Brigadiers took the salute as they marched smartly by with heavy hearts. After several hours they arrived at some wooden huts on the Ecurie Wood road and their first job was to prepare for an inspection by the General Officer Commanding 31st Division. Everyone wished to create a good impression so polishing and cleaning were done extra thoroughly. Though parading on a muddy field was not easy, everything went well, and the new General complimented them on their smartness.

After a short turn in the Line at Vimy Ridge they moved further back to civilisation in the village of Tincques on the St Pol Road. The Signallers were in a small stable built of brick and they had plenty of straw for their beds. There were farmhouses, which supplied omelettes and coffee at reasonable charges, and the Corps Baths were in the village, so they were very comfortable.

When they had been there a few days, Mac, an Irish Officer in charge of the baths, called to see Venables. He was a friend of the family and when in England he had visited Venables' home (just in the same way Venables had 'visited' Barossa), but when Mac went into the Line his nerves gave way, so he was put in charge of the baths.

"Sure, they complain my clean washing is still lousy," he said. "Tell me, what do you think of it?"

"It's clean when you issue it, but it's lousy before the troops get it back to their billets. The lice come out of the uniform and you can't get rid of them," said Venables.

"Sure, that's comfortin'," said Mac.

Constrained by rank, Mac was unable to invite Venables to his billet, but left instructions for him to have as many baths and clean changes of washing as he liked.

8. Backs to the Wall

The 4th Guards Brigade was in general reserve waiting to be thrown into the Line where the enemy's expected attack was fiercest. They were several miles from the Front and only on rare occasions heard the guns. However, on the 21st March they were wakened long before reveille by their thunder; it was more intense than ever before. Very soon it became apparent the battle had commenced under the most favourable conditions for the enemy. Each morning began with a thick mist, which disappeared as the sun increased in power. With weather like this, the battle was again a war of movement, but movement in the *wrong* direction.

A German Infantry Regiment, headed by its band, marching from the Infantry Training School at Sedan having prepared for the Spring Offensive, March 1918. © IWM Q 079590.

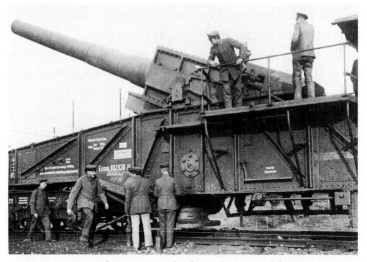

*A German railway gun which took part in the German
Spring Offensive, 1918. © IWM Q 056569.*

They came in touch with the enemy at Ervillers, where
the Battalion dug fresh trenches. Battalion Headquarters
made use of an old gun pit. All the following day they held
the enemy's attack and captured several prisoners. In the
evening the Germans tried to work round the flank, so
Headquarters lined a bank all night with fixed bayonets
and bombs, but the enemy did not attempt to advance
further in the darkness.

Through a mistaken order the Brigade Transport retired
and left them without rations. Permission was given on the
second day to eat half their iron ration, which meant that
for one day they were without food. The next day they had
half a tin of bully and two biscuits.

The next morning, they still held their Line without
artillery support and the following day all were cheered by
hearing the guns were coming back into position. However,
when the guns opened fire, they shelled the Brigade position

instead of the enemy. They inflicted more casualties in an hour than the enemy had done in three days.

To add to the confusion, in the middle of the afternoon a British aeroplane bombed them. At 5pm they were ordered to retire. They'd held the ground against the enemy without full rations. Conversely, their own shells and bombs had blown them out.

They cursed the Germans, the gunners and the transport as they hurried down the valley and over the next ridge, bringing the wounded with them. They were under the enemy's fire all the way, until darkness and the ridge hid them from his view. Eventually, they were told to halt. Worn out, they dropped by the roadside and went fast asleep.

Royal Aircraft Factory B.E. two-seat reconnaissance and light bomber biplane. © IWM Q 069315.

On the 1st April they went to Beinvilliers, where they were able to take off their boots for the first time for twelve days, roll themselves up in two blankets and go fast asleep on a wooden floor. The following morning, they washed, removed twelve days' growth from their faces and hunted lice in their shirts. They cleaned their rifles and equipment and paraded for Commanding Officer's inspection at midday, after the true tradition of the Guards.

About a week later Venables and Stevens were walking in the fields round Tincques on a beautiful April evening. Stevens was comparing the young crops with those at home, until inevitably their conversation gradually passed from the beauties of Spring and the problems of agriculture, to war.

They discussed the enemy's recent success and wondered when and where he would attack again. As they returned to the village, they knelt and prayed in the corner of a field and the simple manliness of Stevens' prayer lifted Venables into the Lord Jesus's presence. They rose from their knees strengthened and encouraged; and after a supper of coffee and omelettes in a farm kitchen, they said goodnight to each other.

Venables took over the last turn of duty at the telephone exchange, passing the time by playing Patience. The others were getting into bed by the light of half a dozen candles arranged round the wall and were discussing the age and beauty of the daughter of the house adjoining their stable. Her mother had wisely kept her out of sight, but some had caught a passing glimpse of her.

The telephone rang and Venables plugged the Brigadier through to the Colonel and listened in to their conversation. When they had finished, he flung down the receiver with an exclamation.

"You said damn, Ven," said Harry.

That's nothing to what you'll say" replied Venables.

"He smokes, drinks, plays cards and now he's swearing. Next, he'll be gambling. He'll soon be as bad as us," said Chick with a twinkle in his eyes.

"He eats the spuds we pinch and sits by our fire made from stolen sticks and clears off when there's trouble," grunted Robo.

"Now Robo! There's no need to be nasty! Ven's all right," said Chick. "Anyway, what's it all about?"

"The Portuguese have run away opposite Hazebrouck and left a gap in the Line that we've got to fill. The lorries will pick us up at 11 o'clock," said Venables. He had hardly

*Battle of Hazebrouck. 6-inch howitzer of the Royal
Garrison Artillery (possibly of the 277th Siege Battery)
being manhandled on to the road and prepared for
towing back to by lorry, near Merris, 12 April 1918. Note
a refugee coming along road pushing a wheelbarrow
piled with his belongings in the background.*
© *IWM Q 008692.*

finished speaking when the bugles, which had sounded 'lights out,' rang in the village street and the Orderly Corporal rushed in. "Parade at once—marching order. Billets to be left tidy."

Battle of Hazebrouck. French refugees from Bailleul, Merris and Meteren in a farm-cart on their way to Cassel passing through Caestre. Note Royal Artillery limbers going in the same direction, 12th April 1918.
© IWM Q 008697.

Approaching Hazebrouck they met streams of refugees, old people, women and children, riding on farm carts or pushing barrows loaded with all their portable belongings. Cattle and pigs jostled with the crowds. The town itself was deserted and the shutters were up at the shops and houses. Hearing the noise of the lorries, the locals who hadn't left came to their doors. Recognising the cap badges they shouted, "Les Gardes, Les Gardes," and waved encouragement.

The Guards stopped at Paradise Farm, but the rest was short lived. They were to hold the enemy at all costs until further reinforcements arrived. If the enemy captured the railhead at Hazebrouck before reinforcements came, then the whole Front would fall back on Paris leaving the Channel ports in his hands.

"Parade at once—fighting order; packs to be left with the transport with one man in charge per section," ordered the Sergeant. "Sarpy, you stop with the packs."

"It's your turn to stop, Ven," said Chick. "Speak up man."

"Sarpy's married with three children, let him stop now he's been told to."

"All right you bloody fool," replied Chick.

The main road was almost impassable in the dark. Pigs were rushing in and out of the traffic, cows were displaying their usual road sense pursued by tired and bewildered refugees. Slow moving horse-drawn carts held up lorries evacuating ammunition and stores, while shells dropped regularly on the crossroads.

The Guards were the only people moving forward against this relentless stream. They threaded their way in and out of the traffic, each man guided by the man in front. Venables recognised the voices of two stretcher bearers who were dressing a man crushed by a lorry while he lay on the grass verge. As Venables marched by he called out, "Goodnight Steve. Goodnight Woodward."

"Goodnight Ven," they replied. We'll be following on in a few minutes."

After marching for some time, they turned right off the main road and, leaving the traffic, continued down a country lane to a farmhouse. Battalion Headquarters set up in the kitchen; the Signallers made use of the haybarn.

The balance of the war was on a knife edge and caused Sir Douglas Haig to make the following statement: "There is no other course open to us but to fight it out. Every position must be held to the last man, there must be no retirement. With our backs against the wall believing in the justice of our cause, each one of us must fight to the end."

Consequently, the 4th Guards Brigade was digging in, each man knowing his life depended on it, but unfortunately, No.1 Company, 3rd Coldstream Guards, was still digging when the enemy opened fire. The men dropped their spades, jumped into the partially completed trenches and seized their rifles and bombs. Going in the opposite direction, stretcher-bearers Stevens and Woodward went at once to assist the wounded. This was their duty, but it made them vulnerable too. Nevertheless, these brave men worked on until German rifles took aim; and Stevens and Woodward went to be with their Lord Jesus.

Back row, left to right: Woodward (stretcher bearer) killed April 1918, Signaller George Venables, Martin Stevens (stretcher bearer) killed April 1918, Cook, (machine gunner), badly wounded March 1918. © Source unknown— original with Venables Family.

A few men of the Northumberland Fusiliers came into the farm and reported that the enemy was working round the Brigade's right flank, so Battalion Headquarters was ordered to fix bayonets. Accompanied by the Fusiliers and under the command of an Officer and the Drill Sergeant, they crossed a field in open order. They were greeted with machine gun fire and field guns firing over open sights. They were ordered to dig in on reaching the opposite hedge, but this could not afford proper cover as the ground sloped the wrong way.

Venables felt for his trenching tool but he had used it for making the fire for breakfast and had left it behind. Bullets whistled and hit the ground all round, while shrapnel burst above their heads with deafening reports and thick black smoke. A Fusilier was digging away with his trenching tool next to Venables. He groaned and fell dead. Venables seized the man's trenching tool and began to dig, but moments later the order was passed down the Line to extend over the hedge to the left.

Chick, Robo and Ven obeyed and found themselves in a flat ploughed field whose furrows afforded much more shelter than the sloping green bank they had left. They took out extra clips of ammunition and spread them on their khaki handkerchiefs. They decided on the range of the hedge opposite. They fixed their sights. They waited with rifles to their shoulders. The situation was desperate, but they resolved to do their best and fight to the last.

The morning wore on and their eyes were fixed on the hedge across the field, but they saw no sign of the enemy. Venables prayed that he might do his duty. Then he prayed for his two comrades. He longed to live as every other soldier did. Whoof! Whoof! The shrapnel kept bursting a little to the right killing comrades who'd remained at the original objective.

After waiting for some time and devastated by the loss of their comrades, Chick, Robo and Ven decided to return to Battalion Headquarters. They got up to run. The enemy's rifles cracked, and bullets whistled by. They were so cramped with lying in one position that they could hardly move one leg in front of the other, but they reached the farm without being hit.

All day long the enemy attacked the Brigade Front in vastly superior numbers. Some of the posts fought until there was not a man left alive. It was decided to re-adjust the position at nightfall and leave the remains of the farm in the hands of the enemy.

Headquarters fell back after dark and eventually settled at Caudescure Farm where a road entered the Nieppe Forest. A telephone wire was run out to Brigade Headquarters and a Signal Office established in the cellar of a cottage.

Venables and Patch were on duty in the cellar when a shell dropped on the cottage. Remarkably, the cellar floor held, and they were unhurt. Meanwhile Chick had killed and dressed some fowls and made a delicious stew of boiled chicken, which was enjoyed by all other ranks at Headquarters.

As time passed, all who were left of the Battalion were billeted in one farm. They were cleaning up their kit and themselves, when the General came into the yard. He called them together round the cooker in an informal way and congratulated them on the action of the previous days. As he contrasted the handful of men with the Battalion he had inspected when they joined the Division, he spoke with emotion and difficulty. This emotion resonated with Venables. The loss of Stevens was a great blow for they had formed a friendship based on a common faith and a common adversity. While they respected their comrades they were unable to share their thoughts with them. Venables felt lonelier than he done since his early days in France.

On the 22nd April the 3rd Battalion Coldstream Guards, having received reinforcements, took over the Support Position from the Grenadiers. Battalion Headquarters occupied a deserted farm. The Signal Office was in a small stable in an out of the way corner. It had the usual telephone exchange with lines to the four Companies, Brigade Headquarters and the Commanding Officer in the cellar of the farmhouse.

Two days later the Battalion took over the Front Line on the edge of the Nieppe Forest with Battalion Headquarters in a sawmill in the woods. The Signallers found an animal's leg on the roadside and discussed if it were a calf or a deer, but they could not decide. It didn't matter. They were hungry. They cut off all the outside and made an excellent steak, which they fried with onions found in a deserted woodsman's cottage.

The enemy continued to push wherever he could by all available means. The paths and road through the wood were shelled with mustard gas. This hung about in the thick undergrowth and was a constant source of danger.

On the second evening the enemy decided to pay special attention to the sawmill and shelled it with high explosives and gas. The Commanding Officer ordered everybody to

German troops fixing cylinders in position in a trench before a gas attack. © IWM Q 055560.

clear out of the canvas huts and look after themselves. Venables sat under a pile of timber with his gas mask on as shells dropped all around. The high explosives burst with a deafening report and the gas shells burst like inflated paper bags. The combination of the two was not pleasant.

On the 27th April they were relieved by the 29th Division. They left the wood by the Le Notte-Hazebrouck Road on a bright moonlight night. They were marching along behind a line of ammunition wagons, when a battery of German guns opened fire on the crossroads. At the sound of the guns, the animals drawing the wagons bolted and the infantry dropped flat in the ditch beside the road. They ducked and ran between the salvos of bursting shells until they were out of the danger area. All the way to Hazebrouck the roadside was strewn with broken carts and dead animals. They all felt more comfortable when they were through the town and were settled in good billets near Hondegham.

Their three week stay at Hondegham was occupied in digging a support line and was uneventful except for the activities of enemy aeroplanes. The aeroplane was now playing a much more important part in the war. It was a new experience to lie in a tent and hear the droning of planes in the early hours of the night, wondering when and where the bombs would be dropped.

Towards the end of May they moved to the very pleasant village of Theivres, a few miles east of Doullens, where they spent a quiet time except for one night's bombing. The second evening after their arrival the Orderly Corporal announced that Venables was to proceed by bicycle to Doullens to meet the Regimental Quartermaster Sergeant. Venables was required to buy beer for the Battalion.

"Buy beer?" said Venables. "What's that got to do with me? What exactly is my duty—to be Corporal, to supply the money, or to roll the barrels home, or what?"

"I don't know," replied the Corporal, "unless you have to taste the various brands and see which is best."

"Him! Taste beer!" said the disgusted Robo.

"He don't know good from bad."

"I thought you said it was all good," rejoined Venables with a grin. "Only some better than others."

"Tell the Quarterbloke you're a teetotaller Ven and I'll go in your place," said Robo.

"When I enlisted I promised to obey the Officers the King set over me," replied Venables.

"Just like the Army to send a teetotaller to buy beer," groused Harry.

"The Army's not so mad as you think," said Venables. "I'm the only one they can trust to taste *and* come back sober."

Next morning Venables set off to cycle to Doullens. It was a bright May morning and the way was through narrow country lanes where wild flowers and birds ensured he forgot about war. On top of the beer run, he had just received a pound note from home. He hoped of securing something extra to eat at the EFC (Expeditionary Force Canteen).

The EFC was a very imposing shop divided into two parts. All the good things were in a part labelled, "Officers' Servants only." He ignored the notice and walked in with the Officers' Servants but was promptly turned out. Ham, tongue and sausages were not intended for Privates, so he had to keep his pound note and be content with a packet of Petit Beurre biscuits. As he left, the Quartermaster came up and said:

"There's no beer in Doullens today, Venables. You can go back."

Venables was somewhat consoled that his disappointment would be as nothing compared with the Battalion's disappointment when they knew there was no beer. He arrived at the billet as tea was being served and was greeted by the obvious:

"When's the beer coming Ven?"

"Not tonight" he replied with a grin. "There wasn't any in Doullens."

"That comes of sending a teetotaller to buy it. They never were any good."

The Battalion moved to Couchie, near La Basque Wood, where the 2nd Battalion was camped. By now, Venables was serving with an old friend called Sibson. In the two Battalions there were men known to Sibson who had frequented the Soldiers' Home at Windsor since Venables had been in France. Sibson and Venables were able to get them together on several occasions in the corner of a field for prayer meetings and Bible reading. Sibson had brought six copies of a small hymn book called Musical Messages so they could sing together, as well.

Despite the guns and all the uncertainty of war they could rest in the unchangeable Word of God. They prayed together, not for their own safety, but for the souls of their comrades who had lost all faith in God. They prayed for friends at home, for peace and for courage in the meantime to do their duty. One of the favourite verses was:

"Like a river glorious in God's perfect peace,
Over all victorious in its bright increase,
Stayed upon Jehovah hearts are fully blest
Finding as he promised perfect peace and rest." [15]

Their simple faith in the God of the Bible whose love was revealed at the Cross of Christ lifted them above the contradictions and injustices of war. Returning one evening from such a meeting Sibson was asleep in his tent when the others returned from the canteen. Stumbling through the door the first man stopped and, pointing to the sleeping soldier said, "He's got something we haven't, look at his face. He always looks so peaceful."

"He gets the wind up like the rest of us," said another.

"Perhaps he does, but he's different," and with this, they all agreed.

---

15 Taken from the hymn by Frances R Havergal (1876), 'Like a River Glorious'.

9. Victory

On July 9th a long train of vans rattled along conveying the 4th Guards Brigade to an unknown destination. It was rumoured that they were going for a long rest at the seaside. The train was taking them further and further from the Front, but they all suspected there was some special and unpleasant task awaiting them.

At midnight they detrained in a siding at Eu and marched to a camp on the hillside. Waking next morning they found they were overlooking a pleasant little bay of

Criel Plage, July 1918 – November 1918.
An ecumenical party after a bathe in the sea.
Back row from left to right: Sibson (Brethren), Venables (Brethren), Young (Methodist), Sambrook (Anglican), and Taylor (Roman Catholic).
© *Source unknown—original with Venables Family.*

the sea at Criel Plage, between La Treport and Dieppe. Here they became a Training School for young Officers.

The Signallers looked after the telephone exchange and when not on duty did signal schemes round the district. Venables, Young and Sibson bathed in the sea most afternoons and finished the day with a coffee and fish supper in the cottage of a Belgian refugee. The news from the Front was very good. The German attacks were finally stopped, and the Allies were again taking the offensive with considerable success.

July and the greater part of August slipped quickly away in these congenial circumstances. About the middle of August, the Brigade was called upon to furnish reinforcements for the Guards Division that was heavily

An escort of the South Staffordshire Regiment bringing German prisoners through Bucquoy, 21st August 1918, following the Battle of Albert at the start of the Hundred Days Offensive. © IWM Q 011219.

engaged in the attack. Headquarters' Signallers were asked to volunteer to take part in the final battle of the war, but, having had enough battles and preferring the seaside to the Front Line, nobody volunteered.

The Sergeant then announced that one of them would have to go and Venables, being the youngest soldier, would be the one. He was held in suspense for some days, but it was finally decided that he was to remain. Sibson and Young were posted to the 2nd Battalion and on the 31st August Venables said goodbye to them. (In October, Sibson was again invalided home. The strain and hardship of the war had been too much for him and they brought on an illness that caused his death a few years after the Armistice.)

Middle row, third from the left:
Guardsman Venables on leave in Paris, 22nd September 1918.
© *Source unknown—original with Venables Family.*

Venables became very friendly with Ginger Birkett, a Cumberland youth employed as the Orderly Room Corporal. He was very boyish in appearance and ways and a typewriter was far more suitable to him than a rifle and a bayonet. In the middle of September, they went to Paris together for eight days' leave.

They stayed at the leave club in the Hotel de la Republique, where the British colony in Paris did its best to give the men a good time. They had been used to canteens where anything was considered good enough for ordinary Tommies but here the motto seemed to be that nothing was too good. The organisation was perfect and the absence of red tape, the air of liberty, the comfort of the well served meals and the softening influence of pure womanhood were a great joy.

First left from the truck: Guardsman Venables on leave in Paris, September 1918. © Source unknown—original with Venables Family.

The days were spent in seeing the sights of the city in the charge of a capable lady conductor and the evenings at concerts, lectures and dances. The eight days passed all too quickly and Venables and Ginger left Paris having had a thorough mental tonic.

Venables and Ginger were informed the Brigade had moved and instead of going to Dieppe they were sent to Peronne. As they approached the Forward Area, which was well behind the original Front Line, every cottage hung out a white flag of some description to show there were no soldiers there. Every village, wood and prominent point, where the enemy's rear guard had made a stand, was marked by groups of bodies in khaki or field grey. The dead lay with their topcoats thrown over them; silent cohorts waiting until the burying parties caught up with the advance.

On the morning of November 11th Dusty was taking a telegram on the telephone. He got into such a state of excitement that he could not write it down.

"Here somebody take this," he said, "I can't. It says the war's over."

Venables picked up the receiver and began to write on the message pad while the others gazed over his shoulder.

"Following from GHQ begins AAA. Hostilities will cease at 1100 hours today. AAA. Our troops will stand fast on the line reached at that hour AAA. There will be no intercourse with the enemy of any description."

In the evening they sat silently round the campfire gazing into its glowing embers without the fear of being bombed and their thoughts found little expression in words. One after another, as the fire died down, they turned into their tents, rolled themselves up in their blankets and were soon asleep. They had often slept to wake up to go over the top, to hold the enemy's advance, to the noise of bursting shells and bombs, or the dreaded sound of the gas alarm. Then they had slept because men needed sleep to live, but now they slept to rest, the rest of peace and security.

Guardsman Venables used this message pad to record the Armistice on 11th November 1918.
© Venables Family.

The Brigade was disbanded and each Battalion rejoined its old Brigade in the Guards Division at Maubeuge. At 8am on the 18th November they commenced the march into Germany. Passing through Houchine and Anderleu they arrived on the third day at Charleroi, one of Belgium's industrial cities.

The Cavalry and the disorganised rabble that was once the German Army preceded them. The inhabitants were overjoyed to see them, having been robbed of all they possessed of any value by the retreating soldiers. The route was lined by cheering crowds and little children ran beside the ranks kissing their hands. They passed numbers of half-starved, released British and French prisoners in rags, some of them sick and wounded, wearily making their way in the other direction.

At the entrance to Charleroi the town officials and the General and his staff stood on a raised platform to take the salute while one of the Guards Regimental Bands played in front of it. All day long the infantry, artillery and supply columns poured in a continuous stream into the city. The inhabitants made a holiday, filling flag-bedecked streets and exhibiting in every shop window articles of copper and brass they had hidden from the enemy.

The Signallers were billeted in an inn at Montigny-sur-Sambre. The proprietor had been in America and spoke English well. He offered them his best bedroom, which they declined, as they were not free from vermin. They slept on the floor of the parlour and agreed that it was the best billet of the War.

Soon after they arrived, they were taken into the cellar and shown the hole where he had hidden his brass, copper and best wines. Having drunk one another's health, he told stories of the ruthless oppression and cruelty of the German occupation. In the evening they joined the crowds that thronged the city streets while the Military Band played in the square.

After two days Venables went on leave, arriving home on the 26th November. He returned from leave and arrived in Cologne a day before the Battalion. They were billeted in a school in Erinfield, which had central heating. Hot baths could be had each morning in the basement. New clothes, uniforms and blankets were issued. After two and a half years, Venables was finally able to say he was the only 'inhabitant' of his shirt. The lice were gone.

At this time, rations were still poor and very little could be bought from the Germans. In fact, they would offer the men ridiculous prices for tins of bully beef or a piece of soap. On Christmas Eve, a flock of sheep was found outside the town. The sheep were slaughtered and served as roast mutton on Christmas Day. It was as tough as leather.

Venables and Ginger spent their free afternoons seeing the sights of the city, including the Cathedral and the famous Rhine Bridge. They could not help contrasting the Cathedral with the beautiful buildings destroyed in France. They were there as conquerors yet were courteous and friendly to the Germans. One evening an article from the Cologne Gazette was read out in the YMCA complimenting the Guards on their gentlemanly behaviour to the civilians. It was a great day when the Division formed up opposite the station to receive the Regimental Colours from England. All civilians had to remove their caps as the Colours marched through the city; those not doing so were arrested.

Venables enjoyed his stay in Cologne, but the purpose for which he had joined the Army was accomplished. He was anxious to return to civilian life. His father wrote to the Commanding Officer saying that he needed him in the business at home. As he had a post to go to, he left on 12th January 1919, with the second party for demobilisation travelling via Dunkirk and Tilbury Dock to Clipstone.

He was given a good character by the Commanding Officer and a document to say that he was free from vermin and infection by the Medical Officer. He was also given a post office order for twenty-two pounds comprising back pay, bonus, a month's ration money and the price of a new suit of clothes.

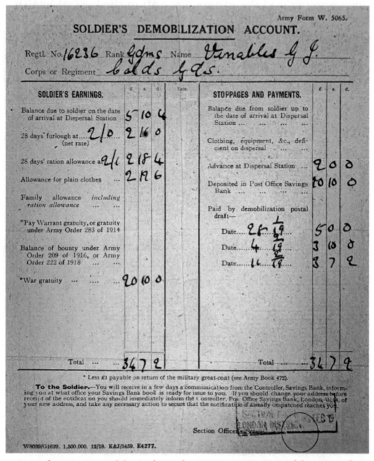

Guardsman Venables' 'demob' account. © Venables Family.

His elder sister who had been in the VAD (Voluntary Aid Detachment) had returned before him, his next brother arrived two hours after him from the Field Artillery and at Easter the family was completed by his brother returning from the Royal Flying Corps and his youngest sister from boarding school. They were all home except for Henry. How thankful they were that out of a family of six, only one was missing and the others were all in the best of health.

A photograph taken at the family home in Stafford in February 1924 following the funeral of Guardsman Venables' father, Henry. Back row, left to right; Sidney Venables (Cadet in the Royal Flying Corps 1918), Guardsman George Venables (Signaller, 3rd Battalion Coldstream Guards), Charles Venables (Initially of the Coldstream Guards at Caterham before being invalided out to the Veterinary Corps). Front row, left to right; Jane Venables (Red Cross Nurse 1914 – 1918), Ellen Venables (Mother) and Nellie Venables (Youngest in the family; she was still at school during World War One).
© Venables Family.

*Red Cross Nurse
Jane Venables,
1917; sister of
Private George
Venables.
© Venables
Family.*

*Cadet Sydney Venables
of the Royal Flying
Corps, 1918; brother of
Private George Venables.
© Venables Family.*

Seven years later Venables went to the unveiling of the Guards War Memorial on the Horse Guards Parade. He walked onto the square in Wellington Barracks mingling with a crowd of men in all kinds of civilian clothes. Some he recognised at once, others had altered so much that he hardly knew them.

"Remember digging us out at Gouzeacourt?" said one.

"Remember Saules Farm, Egypt House, International Corner?" One after another they greeted him, and he greeted them.

"Fall in here 3rd Battalion. Hurry up Gentlemen please."

Venables started and looked round. Yes, it was the Drill Sergeant in bearskin and scarlet, calling them gentlemen and saying please! The long line of civilians fell in under the charge of the Colonel in morning coat and silk hat. They marched out past the Guard following the scarlet and bearskins of the New Army. The Division filled the Horse Guards Parade and moved with the old smartness, greatly helped by receiving the word of command on loudspeakers.

After the ceremony they marched back to Wellington Barracks and were dismissed. As Venables walked out past the Guard he straightened his hat, looked down to see if his buttons were done up and smiled to himself, as he half expected to hear a familiar command "Come here that man" recalling him to face an offended Sergeant Major.

The night train to the north was warm and comfortable. Thoughts of the past, buried for seven years, had been revived in his mind. The injustices of life, magnified a hundred times by war, filled his thoughts until he fell asleep, to dream. The band was playing, the boys were marching, and the ranks were filled with the familiar faces of the dead from a score of battlefields. The Governor, Martin Stevens, Jack Sibson, Woodward, Will Hazlewood, Charlie Mawson and Boxer Brown were with them.

As his dream continued, a voice cried out and said, "These are they which come out of tribulation and have washed their robes and made them white in the blood of the Lamb. Therefore, are they before the throne of God and serve Him day and night in His temple: and he that sitteth on the throne shall dwell among them. They shall hunger no more neither shall the sun light on them nor any heat. For the Lamb which is in the midst of the throne shall feed them and shall lead them to living fountains of water; and God shall wipe all tears from their eyes." [16] The train stopped. He woke with a start.

The war had taken away so many of his friends and yet it had provided him with a home, for he married the young woman who first opened the door to him at Caterham, rewarding 'the brother of substance' for his kindness, by 'stealing' his daughter.

The End

---

16 These words are found in the Book of Revelation 7:14-17 (KJV).

Epilogue

On leaving the Army in January 1919 my father wrote, "I was anxious to show my gratitude to God for his preserving care, when so many of my comrades had been killed."

His home church was equally anxious to find him something to do, so they gave him a Sunday school class to teach twelve-year old girls! However, he soon found a more appropriate avenue of service by helping to run Christian camps for boys, where his Army training was invaluable.

At the same time he was adjusting to civilian life with his two remaining brothers, who were also returning from active service. Together they started to revive a family business which had suffered neglect and underfunding during the war years. Within a generation the business was one of the market leaders in its field.

My father's involvement in Sunday school and youth work developed over the years. He took an active role in training and equipping the teachers for work with all age groups. In 1939 the combined children and youth groups hired a special train for their summer outing. Over 500 tickets were booked.

In the early part of the Second World War my father visited a home where two teenage boys had stopped coming to Sunday school. A distraught mother greeted him saying she could do nothing with the boys and that their father was away in the war. Her plea was, "God bless you sir, if you can help."

This led to the founding of the Holmcroft Youth Club. My father approached the County Youth Officer who welcomed him with open arms and offered the use of a primary school in the locality. After a series of breakages and complaints from the school my father realised how unsuitable it was for a Youth Club. Consequently, land was acquired and a building gradually took shape.

During Fire Watching Duty at his workplace he wrote a paraphrase of the Gospels for reading in the epilogue at the end the Club's evening of activities. This led on to the introduction of an informal Sunday evening service.

Over sixty years later the Club is still running as the Holmcroft Youth and Community Centre. In a booklet that my father wrote to raise funds to level and drain the playing field he said, "If the physical and cultural activities of a youth club are closely interwoven, the spiritual runs through both in a golden thread … It is therefore essential that they should know the only source of an abundant life, through a personal faith in God, as revealed in Jesus Christ."

In 2018, I was interested to learn that my father had given SASRA a copy of his biography. It is my hope and prayer that members of the British Military will read this book and see faith in Christ at work, even in dark and cruel times.

Geoffrey L Venables,
February 2019, West Sussex.

Bringing it all Together[17]

As Guardsman Venables unpacked his life-story for us we probably noticed references to Army Chaplains and para-Church organisations called the Soldiers' Christian Association (SCA) and the Young Men's Christian Association (YMCA). This is instructive; a witness for Christ was possible, in the godless carnage of global war.

Drilling down a bit further, much ink has been used to describe the effectiveness of the Military Chaplain during the First World War. The Medal Role for individual Chaplains speaks for itself and our author saw Chaplains serving on the Front Line and under bombardment, too. Tellingly, at the outbreak of World War One the Army Chaplains Department fielded one hundred and seventeen Chaplains. By August 1918 the number of Commissioned Chaplains was three thousand four hundred and sixteen.

Elsewhere, others were also hard at work for Christ. These men and women didn't wear a military uniform, but, like the Chaplains, they carried a deep concern for the spiritual and moral component of the fighting men.

Leading this work was the YMCA and drawing on experiences from the Boer War the YMCA deployed a cohort of volunteers shortly after hostilities began. Their huts were used as canteens, meeting rooms, chapels and rest centres. By the end of the Great War, the YMCA had deployed over three thousand five hundred workers.

---

17 With thanks to Mark Powell, SASRA Area Representative for North London and the East of England.

In a similar vein the SCA was also able to leave its mark. SCA huts were purposefully evangelistic and those who committed to the mission were Christians who wanted to reach soldiers with the good news of Jesus. Guardsman Venables knew the blessings of the YMCA and the SCA; and many others did, as well.

Although Army Scripture Reader Benjamin Johnson only makes a limited appearance in *The Guardsman* this belies the facts of his time. Found amongst the soldiers at home and abroad, the Army Scripture Reader and Soldiers' Friend Society (ASR and SFS) had been officially serving for Christ since 1838. Its work was essentially evangelistic, but, just like Military Chaplains and others involved in the spiritual aspect of a combatant's life, they had to establish credibility. Consequently, an Army Scripture Reader had to have completed military service prior to becoming a Reader.

During subsequent decades after 1918, the Scripture Readers' work was known by different names as the Army modernised and the Royal Air Force grew. But by God's grace, the mission aim remained the same. In 1950 the name 'SASRA', was forged.

More than one hundred years have passed since Guardsman Venables encountered Scripture Reader Benjamin Johnson in Windsor. Yet despite the passage of time, Chaplains and the Chain of Command continue to graciously permit SASRA's Christian witness to The Guards.

Army Scripture Reader Gavin Dickson completed thirteen and a half years' military service as a soldier with the 1st Battalion Scots Guards before he joined SASRA. Amongst his many roles in the Scot Guards, he was a

Regimental Signaller, just like Venables. As a Scripture Reader in Germany Gavin has providentially engaged with serving and former Guardsmen. He has also ministered to soldiers in the Welsh Guards Band.[18]

Back in England, Army Scripture Reader Lee McDade has permission to labour for Christ at the Army's Infantry Training Centre in Catterick. Over the last six years Lee has met soldiers from all the Guards Regiments: Grenadiers, Coldstream, Scots, Irish and Welsh. While in Aldershot, Army Scripture Reader Jim Henderson continues for the Lord with personnel in the Scots Guards.

In closing, we must conclude that a witness for Christ in the British Military is both historical and contemporary. I'm sure you will join me in giving thanks to God for His grace towards The Guards and wider military family. Please pray that this will always be the case until Jesus Christ returns with a loud command, with the voice of the archangel and with the trumpet call of God.

The Editor
April 2019

---

18 ASR Dickson has been redeployed to Edinburgh.

Supporting SASRA

The work of SASRA is unique within the British establishment. Our uniformed Scripture Readers are permitted to go behind the wire on military units to point men and women to the Lord Jesus Christ. This is a work we have been doing for over 180 years, and while the social and technological context has changed dramatically, the human condition and spiritual needs remain the same. Only the good news of the gospel of Jesus Christ can meet profound human need.

The Association receives no Government or MoD funding. From its beginning the work has relied on support in prayer and financial giving from Christian churches and individuals. We minister amongst mostly young people (the average age of the British Army is twenty-three), many of whom have had no exposure to the Christian faith. The first time most have been in a church building is on their first Sunday in uniform, and the first time they have held (let alone read) a Bible is when they are presented with one after their first service.

Given the challenges that our Armed Forces face: the moral questions around armed conflict and the risk of 'moral injury in the mind' over what they are called upon to do and see, we believe that it is vital that they have a robust Christian witness to equip and prepare them for future duties.

SASRA's Council has tasked the Executive with more than doubling the number of full time Readers, to a team of thirty. This is an ambitious target. Please pray the right candidates would be called by God and be made willing to undergo a challenging selection and training process, as well.

In closing, if you'd like to keep up to date with SASRA, please call HQ on 03000 301302 to find out more about our informative, free publications. Equally, if you are moved to support SASRA financially, please consider 'small and often' by way of Standing Order. A steady income will help HQ make concrete plans for souls behind the wire. Thank you.

Rough Journal

H. WISBEY / SASRA HQ

The inspirational story of
Army Scripture Reader
Harry Wisbey with
the Suffolk Regiment,
Expeditionary Force
August–September 1914

Paperback

Publisher: 10 Publishing;
1st Edition 2014

ISBN 978-1-90961-189-4

£4.00

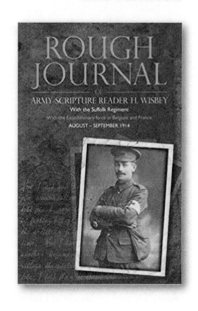

SASRA at the Somme

W. G. RANSLEY

**The War Diaries of
ASR 'Old Bill' Ransley**

ED. SHONA WILKIE

72pp
ISBN 978-1-84625-542-7
Day One Ref SASRAS5427
£6.00

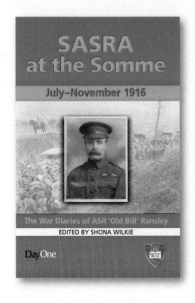

SASRA (The Soldiers' and Airmen's Scripture Readers Association) brings you Old Bill's writings during the Battle of the Somme, from July to November 1916! Old Bill (William Ransley) became an Army Scripture Reader shortly after leaving the army in 1889. Having worked for God in his last six years serving in the army, he decided to dedicate his time and energy to sharing the gospel full time with the men and women of the military. His work saw him sailing off to the hospitals in northern France, where he experienced the bloodbath of the Battle of the Somme through his encounters with injured soldiers from both sides. His journal gives a glimpse of the role of Scripture Readers and sheds light on the message of hope SASRA readers took, and still take, to the men and women of the Armed Forces.

Scripture Reading to the End

ASR William G Ransley and his Gospel witness, France, 1918

ED. BILL NEWTON

100pp

ISBN 978-1-84625-603-5

Day One Ref SCE6035

£6.00

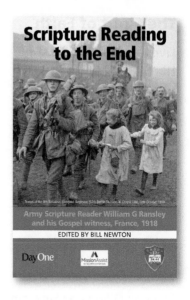

With a deep reliance on and faith in the Lord Jesus Christ, Army Scripture Reader William Ransley takes us into the agony of the Great War and shows us men facing their mortality both with and without Christ. Posted to Boulogne in 1914 and later to the hospitals of Wimereux in Northern France, Ransley faithfully witnessed to those profoundly affected by the war. His honest, gracious testimony and compassion are a challenge to us all. This book takes Ransley's diary and focuses attention on the period when World War One staggered to its brutal and horrifying conclusion in 1918. The need was great: so many souls on both sides, facing a violent entrance into eternity. Yet through it all, Ransley's faith in Christ and unswerving loyalty to speak the truth is the light that shines in encircling darkness.

The Fight of Faith

Lives and testimonies from the battlefield

Compiled and edited by Colonel P Bray and Major M Claydon, SASRA Council.

201pp (Hardback)
ISBN 978-1-95760-890-0
Published by Panoplia
£7.00

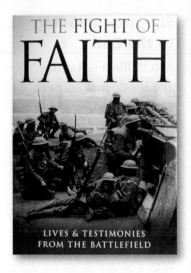

Many an Officer and Serviceman who were committed Christians have testified that they have proved the power of God to keep and help them in their military duty on operations. The Fight of Faith brings together for the first time fifteen such testimonies; from Guardsman to Generals, serving from Malta to Mogadishu in civil and world war. They all found the promises given in The Bible to be true and answers to prayer to be real even in these testing circumstances.

SASRA—
The Lord's Prayer—
Equipping Disciples to Serve

Learning from Jesus how to talk to His Father

PAUL BLACKHAM

With illustrative stories from SASRA Scripture Readers and Area Representatives

ED. SHONA WILKIE

128pp
ISBN 978-1-84625-559-5
Day One Ref SASRALP5595
£6.00

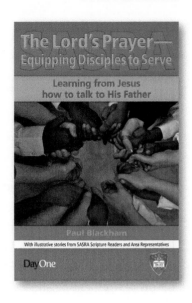

Rev. Blackham and SASRA bring you a study of the basic pattern of the Lord's Prayer, helping you to learn from Jesus, the Eternal Son, how to speak to His Father, who is enthroned in the highest heaven. For messed-up people like us to speak to the most holy Father in the highest level of reality is utterly impossible—but because of Jesus, it is possible. And knowing how to talk to our heavenly Father as Jesus did is the key to knowing life and peace, even in the most terrible circumstances. Each line of the prayer is illustrated through stories told by current Scripture Readers and Area Representatives of encounters with men and women of the Armed Forces as they have seen the outworking of this prayer in SASRA's ministry. May this book encourage you to speak to the Father of our Lord Jesus, and to remember our soldiers, airmen and airwomen in prayer.

Other Publications

Operation Salvation

DAVID MURRAY

96pp
ISBN 978-1-84625-629-5
Day One Ref SASRAOS6295
£6.00

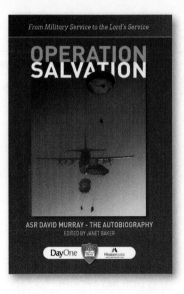

This is a gripping tale of bravado, booze, battles and at times bitter failures. In an action-packed life David Murray escaped dead-end jobs, Glasgow knife-gangs and bullets in Northern Ireland.

His autobiography is a well-paced and plain-speaking account of a man constantly on the move – until the day God Himself finally caught up with him. This is a great book of memories charting Glasgow and Army life in the 60s and 70s. But it's much more than social history.

"It's a wonderful testimony to God's surprising mercy and power in unlikely places and people. A book to read and to give away."
ANDY HUNTER, FIEC Scotland & North of England Director